To my practical, warm, unflappable mother.
You taught me to love the ugly scones,
embrace the broken cookies,
and appreciate the beauty of imperfection.

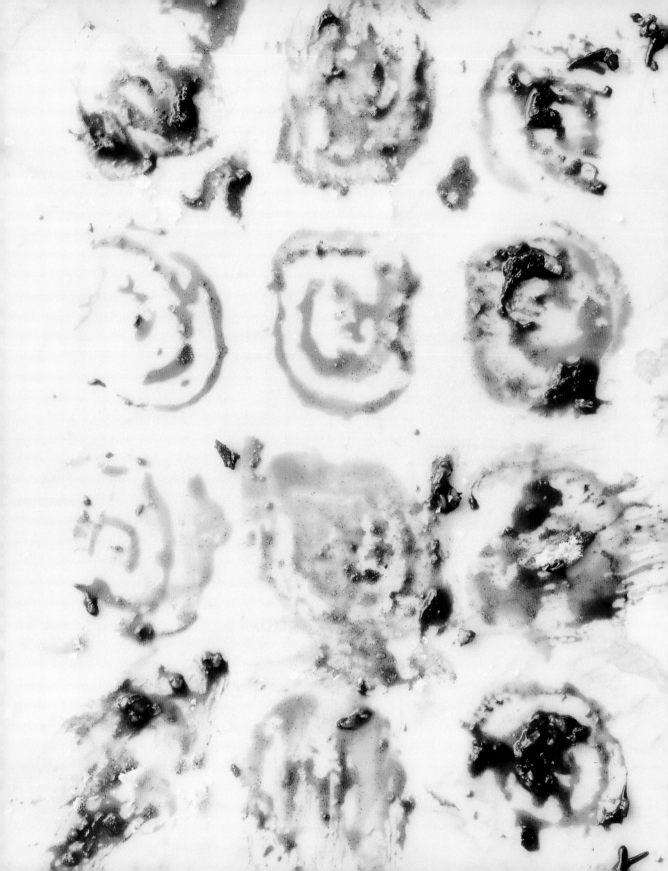

CONTENTS

INTRODUCTION

THE KITCHEN GOD

I stand on a chair pulled up to the counter. My nose hovers near my mother's elbow as I strain to see everything she is doing. She still towers above me. She is God. With a capital G. She knows everything. She *sees* everything, right down to the lone chocolate chip that has strayed from the flock. I have witnessed her rescue burnt cookies and breathe life into an inanimate pile of flour. She is indomitable, and her anger, although rare, is to be feared. I will not talk too much. I will not pester her with questions. I will not touch things until I am told. I will be good, better than I've ever been before, simply because she has answered my prayers and is teaching me to bake.

Her gracious butter tarts shine upon all who eat them and bring them peace—even when you're mad at your sister, who won't stop nudging your foot under the table after you've told her a million million times to stop. The tooth-breaking cookies from the nice ladies at church do not shine. Maybe the church ladies use the wrong flour. But my mother bakes a cupcake so tender, so sweet, so impossibly good, you cannot cry once you put it in your mouth. You can't be mean or angry or even scared. You can choke if you eat it too fast, but I will eat anything we bake today slowly. I will chew each bite a million million times. As long as she teaches me to bake.

Before we begin, she issues her commandments.

> *Assemble all ingredients.*
> *Read the entire recipe—twice.*
> *Always wear an apron.*
> *Don't eat the batter.*
> *Share with the whole family.*

(The last decree makes me wish I were an only child.)
Ready?

She pulls boxes and bags from cupboards above my head, aligning them in order. She reads the recipe aloud and touches each ingredient.

Half a cup butter. Her long, slim fingers tap the parchment-wrapped brick.

One, two, three eggs.

Two cups flour. She rests her hand on a large checkered bag that seems to weigh more than I do.

Clear Pyrex measuring cups with fading red print and a yellow ceramic bowl appear from the cupboards below. She opens drawers and sets a wooden spoon, a nest of metal measuring spoons, and a rubber scraper on the counter. She keeps adding items until there's barely a free spot left. I think I will burst when she produces two aprons. The first she ties snugly beneath my armpits. The hem flutters about my ankles, and if I strain, I can brush the lip of the pocket with my chin. *Don't be silly. Pay attention.* She wraps the second apron around her own waist, and I bounce on the chair in anticipation, plucking at the apron pocket with my fingers. She looks at me. She smiles and pinches my cheek. She knows I am trying, although I see in her eyes that my 5-year-old "best" is not as good as she would like.

We begin. She reads the recipe aloud again, this time explaining its meaning. The baking has begun. To keep my hands to myself, I wrap them in the apron, twisting it tight. When I'm instructed to tip the carefully measured flour into the bowl, I whip my hands free, letting the apron fall back in place, forgotten in the excitement. She then hands me the spoon, and I carve wild circles in the batter, swirling in one spot like a figure skater spinning on the ice. She places her hand on mine and guides my arm. Her grip is gentle but firm, and I can smell the floral perfume of her face cream. She talks me through the motion.

Place the spoon at the back of the bowl, push it down to the bottom of the bowl, and pull it toward you. Now pull it up and out. Slide it back and begin again. Fold gently, so as not to send flour flying. Gently, so you can feel the tug of the batter. How else can you know if it's too thick or too thin?

Fast is for TV commercials.

Fast is for cake mix.

This is homemade.

From scratch.

This is baking.

When my mother turns to check the recipe, I sneak a finger of dough. Without looking up from the page, she warns me there will be nothing left to bake if I continue. I resist further transgressions only because I know she will move swiftly from gentle warning to strict punishment. Another stolen bite and I will be sent to my room. I love the raw dough more than baked cookies, but the thought of being exiled from the kitchen makes my eyes fill with tears. This culinary threat alone keeps me in line.

Together we drop the cookies. She scoops the dough while I scrape the lump from the spoon onto the baking sheet. *Not too close. They need room to spread.* How do you know how much room to leave? How can you tell when they're done? When they're cool enough to handle? Cool enough to eat?

The questions tumble out of me faster than she can answer. To silence me, she hands me the dough-covered spoon. This morsel occupies me for several minutes. Determined to get every scrap, I lick so hard, my tongue hurts from the friction. Euphoric that I ate every speck, I am immediately deflated. She performed a minor miracle while I was distracted and scraped the bowl so clean, you'd swear it had never been used. *Time to wash up.* Why do we have to wash the bowl? *Because it's dirty.* How do you know it's dirty when it looks so clean? But she knows. She knows everything.

While the cookies bake, she helps me return the kitchen to its pristine, prebaking state. She washes. I dry and put away. Without looking, she tells me where the measuring spoons live and where to return the bowl. Each item has its own spot. *Bottom cupboard, second shelf, far right, beside the Dutch oven. Middle drawer, at the front, between the grapefruit spoons and corn picks.* She is indeed the Kitchen God, restoring order where chaos once reigned, feeding the masses and healing the pain of terminal curiosity.

My mother is the Kitchen God. She raised a Messy Baker. Her wisdom still astounds me.

This is for you, Mom. Live long and bake.

THE MESSY MANIFESTO

Never trust a person with a clean kitchen.

Baking is a messy art. Chemicals react, dough spills over the sides of the pan, egg whites fly from the bowl, flour finds its way into the utensil drawer . . . halfway across the room from the baking counter.

And if the results are imperfect, all the better. Delicious cake doesn't need a raffia bow, the best cookies are a bit lopsided, and the pie with the filling oozing down the side is the one to pick. After all, it has filling to spare.

Forget the cook in the crisp, hospital-white apron. Instead, look for the person with the chocolate splatter on her cuff, the smudge of flour on her forehead, the fingers stained with berry juice. If her kitchen is messy, it means she's baking. It means she's creating. That she's alive.

Be messy with me.

THE RULES

While I know my way around a stand mixer, I tend to be impulsive and rush things. I come across a delicious flavor combination or get an idea and I want to make it *now*. Not when the butter has softened. Not when the oven has heated. I want to mix and whip and stir, not organize and plan. As a result, I make more than my share of mistakes. And you know what? About 90 percent of my baking disasters could have been avoided if I'd followed these simple rules, which I learned the hard way.

1. BE PATIENT. Baking takes time. The more you rush, the more you ruin. Some recipes come together quickly, some can be done in stages, some take a lot of commitment. It's all doable if you block off enough time. But how much time will you need? A lot depends on the person. I've baked with a friend who scooped cookies so slowly, I nearly shoved her out of the way. My mom can scoop cookies faster than I can eat them, which is pretty fast. So instead of providing specific time allotments, I've assigned each recipe a Commitment Level.

The recipes are:

- ***READY IN AN HOUR OR LESS:*** These recipes can be out of the oven in 60 minutes or less.

- ***DONE IN STAGES:*** You can make these recipes in short stages over time.

- ***LAZY SUNDAY AFTERNOON:*** These recipes take a bit longer but are worth the time.

2. READ THE RECIPE—ALL OF IT—FIRST. If, like me, you struggle with Rule #1, this will be a challenge. My brain says, "Isn't looking at the picture and skimming the ingredient list enough?" No, Brain. It's not. I've had cakes rise out of the pan and spill onto the oven floor because I didn't read the pan size before starting. I have produced soggy-bottomed pies because I failed to lower the rack when preheating the oven. All avoidable.

3. SET OUT YOUR INGREDIENTS BEFORE YOU START. More than once I have gotten halfway through a recipe only to find I am out of an ingredient. Again, I refer you to Rule #1. Take the time to place all ingredients on the counter before you start. Heck, go one step further and *measure* the ingredients to make sure you have enough. The French call this *mise en place.* My mother calls it common sense. Over the years, I have learned that you can't tell just by looking if a big cardboard box of baking soda is full or empty. And someone, we don't know who, might have eaten that bag of chocolate chips you bought last week. We won't discuss the milk situation, but I think you get the picture.

4. USE THE RIGHT INGREDIENTS. The number one reason recipes don't turn out is that bakers altered the ingredients without understanding how the change would affect the outcome. If a recipe calls for sour cream, all-purpose flour, and white sugar, don't be surprised when your soured milk, whole wheat flour, and honey version is heavy and inedible. If, while executing Rule #3, you notice you are out of an ingredient, see page 233 for emergency substitutions.

5. JUDGE WITH YOUR MOUTH, NOT YOUR EYES. Looks can be deceiving. I've choked down artfully decorated dry-as-sand sugar cookies and gobbled delicious appetizers that looked like they came out of the hind end of a donkey. If your cake is too embarrassing to serve, cut it up in the kitchen and deliver it in bowls. If the taste and texture are good, no one will care.

Now that we understand each other, let's begin.

THE BASICS

Sure, I love my food processor and my stand mixer. I use them enough to warrant replacing them immediately should they break. However, I baked without such machines for decades. And you can, too. Don't feel you have to buy expensive equipment if you can't afford it or don't have space. No dedicated baker ever let a lack of equipment stand between them and dessert.

CAN'T-DO-WITHOUT ITEMS

I'm a gadget freak. I've been known to create a new recipe just as an excuse to buy a specific kitchen item that was high on the cool factor and low on versatility. Having given away a lot of these frivolous items, I'm more judicious in my recommendations. You don't need every item in the cooking section of Sears. These, however, are the things you'll definitely need.

APRON: I owned a dozen and never wore them, because they didn't fit or were too hard to adjust. As a result, I have a lot of stained shirts in my closet. Since I also garden, these splattered garments get worn—outside in the vegetable patch. But being the best-dressed gardener on the block is expensive. Unless you have clothes to burn (sometimes literally), I recommend a full apron. Try it on before you buy it. Move about in it. Pretend you're putting a cake in the oven or reaching for vanilla from the top shelf of your pantry. If you like the apron, chances are you'll wear it. If you don't, you've just bought a really expensive piece of fabric and put the rest of your wardrobe at risk.

BAKING SHEETS: You don't have to buy expensive insulated pans or special cookie sheets. Rimmed baking sheets are versatile and can be used for cookies, scones, galettes, and more (even roast chicken). Sure, you'll squish the odd cookie against the side, but those imperfect ones are a reward for the cook. Flimsy baking sheets tend to burn the bottom of cookies. Heavy, light-colored sheets work best, but if you already own pans, you don't need to buy new ones, even if they burn cookies. Just stack two together and line the top one with parchment or a silicone mat. They'll insulate like one of the high-end ones. Once you know which pans you use most, you can invest in good-quality baking sheets.

BOWLS: You can't have enough mixing bowls or enough sizes of them. Stainless steel bowls are the most versatile, because they are light and unbreakable and warm up and cool down quickly. They are also nonreactive, which means you can put acidic items in them. Glass or ceramic mixing bowls are heavy but worth owning in a couple of sizes. Like stainless, they're nonreactive, but they can go in the microwave to boot.

CAKE PANS: You will go broke and run out of storage space long before you acquire all the different shapes and sizes of pans available. Keeping it real, the vast majority of recipes call for only a few standard sizes. Most bakers need:

> *9 × 5–inch loaf pans (1 or 2)*
> *8 × 8–inch square pans (2 or 3)*
> *9-inch round pans (2 or 3)*
> *9 × 13–inch rectangular pan*
> *10-inch tube pan*
> *12-cup muffin pans (1 or 2)*

If you don't have the pan size called for, see "Adjusting Cake Pan Size" on page 232.

COOLING RACK: For years my mom cooled cookies on tea towels topped with a sheet of waxed paper. I thought everyone did this. Turns out she just never had enough cooling racks. While her method is a handy trick in a pinch, cooling racks allow baked goods—everything from cookies and cakes to breads—to cool faster, keep the bottoms from getting soggy, and allow for drainage when you glaze things like Blueberry-Lime Cornmeal Muffins (page 85). If you have more money than space, expandable cookie racks are handy.

DRY MEASURES: When it comes to measuring dry ingredients like flour, these scooplike measures are more accurate than the cup-style measures used for liquids. Just be sure not to use them as scoops, because this can compact flour by as much as 30 percent and put all your hard work to waste. Instead, spoon the flour into the measure and level it off with a knife or spatula.

MEASURING CUPS: These are best for measuring liquids. I like glass ones best because they can go in the microwave if you need to melt butter or warm milk. Plastic measuring cups are lightweight and dishwasher-safe, but some brands can't go in the microwave or handle the extreme heat of boiling water.

MEASURING SPOONS: These range from $1/8$ teaspoon to 2 tablespoons. I use all the sizes in my set, even the spoons at either end of the spectrum. Look for a set with long, sturdy handles and slim bowls. You want them to fit into small spice jars and reach to the bottom of tall containers. I use mine so much that I have two sets— one for liquid measure and one for dry. Is this overkill? Not at all. A leftover drop of vanilla extract has gummed up my dry spices and baking powder often enough to warrant this kind of duplication.

MESH STRAINER: I own a variety of sizes. Small ones are handy for clump-prone baking soda and cocoa, while larger ones are useful for confectioners' sugar and flour. Fine mesh lets only liquid through, so it's perfect for straining lumpy sauces, salvaging crystallized caramel sauce, or obtaining velvety custards. Medium is best for thick purees. Coarse is ideal for draining large items like pasta. I prefer metal strainers because they can handle hot items and are sturdier than their plastic counterparts. Models with long handles keep your hands at a safe distance when working with hot liquids. A round, footless strainer is the most versatile, as it can sit comfortably over bowls.

MICROPLANE: This item is extremely useful. I use it to zest lemons, oranges, and limes. I also grate chocolate, hard cheeses, cinnamon sticks, nutmeg, and fresh garlic. Be warned, though: It can also shred fingers, so be careful when grating small, hard-to-grip items like nutmeg.

MUFFIN PANS: These are useful for more than just muffins. I use my 12-cup tin for cupcakes, appetizers, and even tarts. A 24-cup tin is handy if you like bite-size treats.

OVEN MITTS: Please, please, please, please, please do not use a folded-up tea towel like they do on TV. Please. I have done this. It's not smart. If the towel is a bit damp, you'll risk being scalded. If it's dry, you can still get burned. Or it can catch on fire. Get a set of good, heavy-duty oven mitts, preferably washable ones.

PARCHMENT PAPER: Because parchment is treated with silicone, your baking won't stick. As an added bonus, parchment eliminates the need to grease, so your baking sheets last longer and are easier to clean up—if they need cleaning at all. Through the course of writing this book, I went through three rolls of parchment and washed a baking sheet maybe once. Another bonus: Culinary parchment is biodegradable and compostable.

PASTRY BRUSH: While I love silicone mats and spatulas, I'm not a fan of silicone brushes. They just smear things around without providing much control. I prefer a small, natural-bristle brush for applying egg wash with accuracy. Larger ones are good for dusting flour from pastry or countertops.

PIE PLATES: I use the standard 9-inch glass pie plates with sloped sides. You know, the kind your grandmother used. No need for fancy porcelain. Plus, glass is transparent, so you can see when your crust is cooked.

PLASTIC WRAP: I know it's not environmentally friendly, but plastic wrap is extremely useful. Placed directly on the surface of sauces and custards, it prevents a pesky skin from forming. It makes rolling slice-and-bake cookies a breeze and keeps odors out of butter. Keep it away from the microwave and you're golden.

POTS: Many baking recipes have a stove-top component. Good-quality, heavy-bottomed stainless steel pots are your best bet. Nonstick is good for a lot of things, but if you like to make caramel, the dark interior won't allow you to gauge the color of the sugar, which is crucial. I learned the hard way that nonstick is not caramel-friendly. Must-haves include:

> *10- to 12-inch skillet with lid*
> *1-quart saucepan with lid*
> *2-quart saucepan with lid*

RESEALABLE FREEZER BAGS: Not only can these double as makeshift piping bags (see page 30), they come in handy for chilling pastry, freezing bricks of butter, and sealing leftover baked goods.

SPOONULA: This is a silicone scraper and a spoon rolled in one. I use mine in place of a wooden spoon for soft batters because I can stir, fold, and scrape without having to change utensils.

WHISK: You'll likely need two—a narrow sauce whisk (also called a French whisk) and a big fat balloon whisk. Look for a whisk that is 10 to 12 inches long and feels comfortable in your hand. The sauce whisk is ideal for sauces and custards. It can also blend dry ingredients, lightly beat eggs, and stir liquids together. Don't have an electric hand mixer? You can always beat egg whites and whip cream by hand with a balloon whisk. Think of all the calories you'll burn.

NICE-TO-HAVE ITEMS

These small items are affordable, handy, and worth owning if you bake a lot. Keep in mind that gadget collecting can be addictive. If you can't trust yourself to buy only the ones you need, bring a friend. A *real* friend, not an enabler.

1-TABLESPOON COOKIE SCOOP: A small cookie dough scoop is perfect for making uniform cookies. Not only does the scoop create consistency, which reduces the chance of burning, it saves you time. No more rolling dough into little balls. This scoop is also handy for forming chocolate truffles, making melon balls, and exercising portion control with ice cream. My mother, who thought these were "frivolous," borrowed mine so often, I bought her one in self-defense.

¼-CUP COOKIE SCOOP: Bigger scoops of ice cream are only one reason to buy this. If you've got a 12-cup muffin pan, this will produce round-topped muffins and uniform cupcakes. No more shuffling batter from the overfilled cup to the underfilled one.

BENCH SCRAPER: This stainless steel scraper is the easiest way to remove stubborn pastry dough stuck to the work surface. It's also handy for dividing pastry dough and gathering up small items, like nuts, that scatter when chopped.

ELECTRIC HAND MIXER: If you already have a stand mixer, you don't need this. But if you are new to baking, an electric beater is a good idea, especially if you have weak wrists like I do. Buy the best you can afford. Fluffy icing and light-as-air cakes will be your reward.

FOOD PROCESSOR: If you're going to get one, be sure to get a model with a large capacity and different size bowls. I use the small bowl often for mixing everything from frangipane (page 169) to mayonnaise (page 207). The large bowl is ideal for quick and easy scones.

OVEN THERMOMETER: Most home ovens are off by as much as 50°F. Even if your oven is perfectly calibrated, opening the door can lower the temperature by 25°F. This kind of fluctuation can ruin baked goods. A $10 oven thermometer can solve the problem. Just hang it from the rack at the back of the oven and check its reading against your oven's setting. If your oven is off by a few degrees, adjust the oven temperature accordingly.

TIP: Most modern ovens come with a setting called convection baking. A fan built into the back wall of the oven keeps the hot air circulating so that you can bake more than one rack at a time. Convection cooking requires the baking temperature to be reduced by 25°F. Some ovens require you to manually reduce the temperature, while others do the adjustment for you. Read the manual to be sure you know how your oven works. While convection baking is wonderful for small, individual items like cookies, it doesn't work for large items like a cake or large pan of squares. Use the convection setting on your Boozy Chocolate Torte (page 131) and the sides will crisp while the center remains gooey.

PIE SERVER: If you've ever tried to serve pie with a knife, you know this will help. If you eat a lot of pies, move this item up to the "Can't Do Without" section.

ROLLING PIN: Sturdy doughs like those for yeasted cinnamon buns roll best with a heavy pin with handles. A tapered French rolling pin is ideal for most pie dough and soft cream cheese doughs since you can control the pastry better with the angled edge.

SILICONE MAT: This reusable pan liner prevents baked goods from sticking and can usually be wiped clean with a damp cloth. If yours is greasy, just wash it in warm, soapy water.

SPRINGFORM PANS: These often come in sets and are indispensable for baked cheesecakes. Even if you aren't a cheesecake fan, this style of pan is often called for when making cakes, deep-dish pies, and frozen desserts.

TIMER: Smartphones are making this item less essential, but if you don't have a smartphone, a $10 timer can save your $20 dessert. Sure, you can also use the stove's timer, but when you leave the room, can you hear it? I've proven more than once that I can't.

I'M-A-BAKER-AND-I'VE-EARNED-IT ITEMS

There is no end to the specialty items an addicted baker can acquire. Madeleine tins, sunflower-shaped Bundt pans, kugelhupf pans (I'm not making this up), rabbit-shaped cookie cutters, heart-shaped waffle irons, and pizzelle presses are just a few of the things you can spend your baking budget on.

Back to reality. The following "upgrades" are useful for most avid bakers.

CANDY THERMOMETER: This is a must for certain candies and caramels, yet for some reason, candy thermometers scare people. They shouldn't, since they take the guesswork out of fudge, toffee, cooked frostings, and even preserves. They also ensure you are in the right temperature zone when adding warm water to yeast. Not too hot, not too cold, just right.

PASTRY BOARD: Growing up, I thought everyone rolled pastry on a flour-permeated linen tea towel. I assumed the subtle texture the towel left behind was integral to the final dish. Turns out, using a tea towel was just a trick my mother got from her mother, who likely used what was on hand during the Great Depression. Today I have a wooden pastry board dedicated to the task. It rolls dough beautifully but without the texture marks, which don't make a difference after all. If you are tempted to substitute the wooden cutting board you use for prepping dinner, think twice. Flavors can transfer. Trust me. Onion-infused pastry for a peach pie won't be a big hit.

PIPING BAGS AND TIPS: Disposable bags keep the mess factor down, allow you to pipe multiple colors of icing, and require no cleanup. They are not, however, good for the environment. I rarely pipe anything, so I don't feel too guilty about the occasional disposable bag I send to the landfill. I also have some alternatives using items you have on hand. (See page 30 on how to use parchment and sandwich bags.)

RAMEKINS: The $1/2$-cup size is ideal for crème brûlée, individual fruit crisps, and soufflés. Once you start baking with ramekins, you'll find lots of other uses.

STAND MIXER: In addition to the standard beaters, most come with a whisk, dough hook, and paddle, which is all you really need. If you want to splurge, an extra bowl is a good idea.

ESSENTIAL INGREDIENTS

The ingredients in my pantry are like gases. They expand to fill the available space. As soon as the last few drops of vanilla disappear, two bottles of hazelnut extract rush to fill the gap. When I exhaust my supply of chocolate chips, their cappuccino-flavored counterparts say it's their turn. While collecting unique baking supplies is inspiring, those four kinds of coconut flakes aren't much use when you're out of flour or sugar. The following items are key to baking. If you're confused about what you really need and why, this section will help you stock a practical and versatile baking pantry.

Flours and Thickeners

I could get all technical on you and talk about the percentages of protein each flour contains, but if it's not marked on the package, why would you need to know this? Here's a list of common gluten flours and how to use them.

ALL-PURPOSE FLOUR: This is the most common flour in the home kitchen. It works for most quick breads, cookies, cakes, and pie crusts. As if that isn't good enough, it doesn't require sifting before measuring. *Unbleached all-purpose flour* is cream colored and available in a whole wheat version. Either can be used cup for cup to replace regular all-purpose flour. I prefer regular unbleached all-purpose flour, as it provides the versatility of all-purpose but hasn't been as processed.

> **What to use it for:** pie pastry, cakes, cookies, breads, muffins, and scones (almost any baked good)

> **Not a good substitute in:** angel food and very delicate pastries, as they will be heavier and less tender

BREAD FLOUR: This has a higher protein content (and therefore higher gluten content) than all-purpose flour. It delivers elasticity and a chewy texture. Variations include whole wheat, multigrain, and white (both bleached and unbleached). Bread flour doesn't need sifting and can be replaced cup for cup by all-purpose flour if needed.

> **What to use it for:** yeast breads, hearty pizza dough, and pastries that need structure, such as strudel and Danish pastry

> **Not a good substitute in:** cakes and cookies, as it makes them dry and tough

CAKE AND PASTRY FLOUR: Also known as soft flour, this is made from soft white wheat and has a low gluten or protein content. If your cake calls for all-purpose flour, it's likely because the cake and pastry flour can't support the other ingredients, such as melted chocolate or sour cream. Always sift this flour before measuring, even if the recipe doesn't call for it.

> **What to use it for:** light cakes, delicate pastries, angel food cakes, and white cakes

> **Not a good substitute in:** quick breads and breads and pastries that need structure

WHOLE WHEAT AND WHITE WHOLE WHEAT FLOUR: These contain the entire wheat berry, which includes the bran and wheat germ. They're higher in fiber than white flours and have a nutty flavor. Because they absorb more moisture, they can make your dish dry if you substitute them for white flour. However, they combine nicely with all-purpose and bread flour, so you will often see small amounts called for in cakes, cookies, muffins, and breads.

What to use it for: breads, muffins, and quick breads (usually in combination with other flours)

Not a good substitute in: light cakes and delicate pastries

CORNSTARCH: While this is not a flour, it's often used in baking to lighten the flour or thicken berry desserts without being gummy. I use it in pancakes, waffles, and Dutch babies to help keep them light and airy.

Shelf Life

White flour usually lasts a year from the manufacturing date. Because of the fat from the wheat germ, whole grain and whole wheat flours last only 6 to 9 months and will go rancid if stored at room temperature. If you are not going to be using the flour right away, store it in the freezer to extend the shelf life. Otherwise, keep flour in a cool, dry place. An airtight container works best, but if you go through flour quickly, storing it in the bag it comes in works just fine, too.

Measuring Flours

Growing up, my mother had one set of Pyrex measuring cups. That was it. She used them for everything from flour to milk. Her recipes turned out just fine. However, the more accurate way to measure flour is with a dry measure. Spoon flour into a dry measure and then level it off with a knife or spatula. Scooping with the measure compacts the flour and will throw off your measurement. This excess can make your baked goods dry.

Sugars

Sugar is more than a sweetener. It provides structure, retains moisture, makes the baked good tender, and caramelizes for a depth of flavor artificial sweeteners just can't deliver. While caramelization tastes good, it also helps baked goods gain a remarkable, deep nuttiness. When sugar is enjoyed in moderation and with a good toothbrush at hand, there's no need for artificial sweeteners.

Like flour, sugar comes in many different forms, each with its own unique qualities. See the following page for varieties.

BROWN SUGAR: Whether light or dark, brown sugar is white sugar with molasses added back in. The more molasses, the darker the sugar. Because of its high moisture content, brown sugar can dry out and turn to sweet concrete if not properly sealed. To prevent this, store brown sugar in an airtight container with a terra-cotta sugar disk. If your brown sugar is already rocklike, it can be softened with a half minute in the microwave. Be sure to break up any lumps before you bake with it, since they won't dissolve.

CONFECTIONERS' SUGAR: Sometimes called icing sugar or powdered sugar, this is granulated sugar ground to a powder with some cornstarch added. As the name suggests, it's used for icing, but it can also be used in cookies or whipped cream when a bit more structure is needed.

DEMERARA: This coarse, moist, dark brown sugar can be used in place of regular brown sugar. It has a more intense flavor and provides a butterscotch undertone. I love it for rustic baking.

GRANULATED SUGAR: This is good old white table sugar—the kind you put in your coffee or sprinkle on cornflakes. If a recipe simply says "sugar," this is what it means. However, some recipes call for "granulated sugar" to differentiate it from another kind of sugar used in the same recipe. If stored in an airtight container, granulated sugar keeps pretty much forever. (I think. I wouldn't really know; the turnover at my place is high, given I'm assigned cake duty for all birthdays and holidays and special occasions and rainy days and Mondays . . .)

SUPERFINE SUGAR: Finer than granulated, it dissolves into batter easily and produces a very fine crumb. If you don't have superfine sugar on hand, put granulated sugar in the blender and give it a whirl to powder it before adding it to the recipe.

TURBINADO: A light brown, coarse sugar, turbinado is used mainly for finishing. It's often sprinkled on top of cookies, galettes, and muffins for a crunchy finish.

VANILLA SUGAR: Vanilla sugar is common in European baking but hard to find in North America. Fortunately, it's easy to make. See page 39 for two recipes for vanilla sugar.

Measuring Sugars

Measuring white sugar: While it's hard to compact granulated sugar, confectioners' sugar is another story. Treat it like flour. Spoon the confectioners' sugar into a measuring cup, then press the flat edge of a knife or spatula against the cup's rim to level it off.

Measuring brown sugar: Whether you're using dark, light, or Demerara, brown sugar is usually packed. Scoop the sugar into a dry measure and press it into the scoop with the heel of your hand or the back of a spoon. When you turn the sugar out of the measure, it should hold its shape.

Other Sweeteners

CORN SYRUP: Relax. The type of corn syrup you get in the store is not the dreaded high-fructose corn syrup everyone is flapping about. While far from a health food, it's useful in baking because it provides structure and can be heated past the boiling point.

GOLDEN SYRUP: Also called treacle, this is the richer, more flavorful British version of corn syrup. Look for it in glass jars or tins beside the corn syrup in major supermarkets. Baking shops will also carry it.

HONEY: Like sugar, honey provides sweetness and moisture to baked goods. Unlike sugar, honey varies widely in taste. Depending on where the bees live and what they eat, the honey can take on distinct flavors that might be lost against the other flavors in the baked good. Liquid honey might not have *terroir,* but it's easy to pour and measure. Because honey has a slight acidity, many recipes call for a bit of baking soda to counterbalance this.

MAPLE SYRUP: The boiled sap of sugar maple trees, this sweetener comes in various grades and colors. It takes a whopping 40 gallons of sap to produce 1 gallon of syrup. No wonder it's so pricey. Imitation maple syrup is more affordable but doesn't compare. The darker the syrup, the more maple flavor. Unlike other sugars, once opened, maple sugar needs to be refrigerated or it will go moldy.

MOLASSES: I use fancy molasses, which isn't really all that fancy. Readily available in the grocery store, this mild molasses, also called light molasses, adds sweetness and flavor to your baking, working nicely with spices like ginger and cloves. Dark molasses and light molasses can be used interchangeably, depending on your preference and the spicing of the baked goods. However, intense blackstrap molasses is too bitter and can easily overpower cookies or loaves. Despite being unsuitable for baking, a jar of blackstrap molasses still has a place in the kitchen. It adds depth to slow-cooked dishes like baked beans, barbecued meats, and pulled pork.

Measuring Syrups and Honey

Measuring sticky liquid sweeteners can be messy. Spray or wipe the measuring cup or spoon with oil before you pour in the honey, syrup, or molasses. It will slide out easily, ensuring you don't miss a drop. If your recipe calls for oil or melted butter, save yourself the trouble and measure it first, then use the same cup or spoon to measure the liquid sugar.

Rising Agents

Rising agents, also called leaveners, help bread and baked goods rise. While they don't go rancid, they can lose their potency. That 10-year-old jar of baking powder isn't going to cut it (or rise it). But time isn't the only enemy. Because moisture activates baking soda and baking powder, be sure the measuring spoon you dip into the canister is dry. Many bakers keep two sets of measuring spoons (one for wet ingredients, one for dry) just for this reason.

BAKING POWDER: Most baking powder is double-acting, which means it starts working the second it hits moisture and kicks into action again with the heat of the oven. It's used in recipes where there isn't acid. Because moisture activates this leavener, cakes and muffins with baking powder should go into the oven as soon as they are ready. Don't leave them sitting about or they might sulk. Store baking powder in a cool, dry place for up to 1 year.

> **Test:** Not sure if your baking powder is still potent? Add 1 teaspoon baking powder to $1/2$ cup hot water. If it bubbles, it's active. If it doesn't, you need to buy a fresh supply.

BAKING SODA: Alkaline by nature, baking soda is often used in place of baking powder when there's chocolate, buttermilk, or lemon juice in the batter to balance the acidity. Store in a cool, dry place for up to 1 year.

> **Test:** Add 1 teaspoon baking soda to $1/4$ cup white vinegar. It should foam and hiss. If not, use the remaining baking soda to freshen the air in your fridge and buy another box for baking.

YEAST: By definition, yeast is a live, single-celled microscopic organism that gobbles the flour and sugar in the dough. In return for the meal, the yeast produces carbon dioxide, which makes the dough rise. (Don't overthink this one.) All you need to know is that yeast is very much alive and, as such, needs a nurturing environment. It can be inadvertently killed if not provided the necessities of life.

While there are lots of different kinds of yeast, I use two kinds in this book. Both look like tiny seeds and come in either premeasured packages or small jars. Both are available in the baking section of the grocery store. Both work perfectly well in the home kitchen. If you buy the premeasured packages, store them in a cool, dry place. If you buy the jars, refrigerate or freeze a jar once you open it. Regardless of the expiration date printed on the packaging, use an opened jar within 4 months.

Active dry yeast: This is mixed in warm water to activate it. The water should be between 105° and 110°F. You can test using a candy thermometer, but if you put a (clean) finger into the water, it should feel pleasantly warm, not hot. You'll kill the yeast with water that's 140°F or hotter. If this happens, your bread dough won't rise and kittens will cry. Recipes calling for active dry yeast usually require two rises.

Instant dry yeast: Sometimes called quick-rising, this yeast has slightly smaller granules than active yeast but can be mixed directly into the flour without adding it to water first. It also halves the rising time. So why would anyone use active yeast when instant is faster and easier? A slow rise from active yeast is essential to developing flavors in some dough, such as Crispy-Crust Pizza (page 156).

Don't have the kind of yeast the recipe calls for? See page 234 for substitutions.

Eggs

Flour usually gets top baking billing, what with the cakes and pastries and breads. But I'd argue eggs are more important—overall. You might not need them for pizza dough, but when you look at the big picture, they're culinary miracles in a shell. Eggs give custards form, make light-as-air meringues possible, act as emulsifiers for mayonnaise, keep fillings in check, and add a rich flavor to baked goods.

Size Matters

All the recipes in this book use large eggs. It doesn't matter if they're brown, white, speckled, free range, organic, or omega-3-infused. It doesn't matter if they are in plastic containers or cardboard. All that matters is that they are large, fresh, and at room temperature and have no cracks.

Quick Warmup

If you're like me, you don't always have the time (or patience) to allow refrigerated eggs to come to room temperature unaided. You can speed things up by placing the eggs in a bowl of hot, not boiling, tap water. If it's too hot for your finger, it's too hot for the eggs. Once in warm water, the eggs should be ready to use in a minute or two.

TIP: If you need whites but won't use the yolks right away, cover the yolks in cold water and pop them back in the fridge. Drain the water before using the yolks.

Beating Egg Whites

Leave it to eggs to be challenging. They separate best when cold, but the whites provide the best volume when beaten at room temperature. They refuse to cooperate at the merest speck of fat or grease and sulk on humid days. If egg whites give you trouble, follow these steps:

PERFECTLY BEATEN EGG WHITES

1. Don't whip whites on a humid day.

2. Unseen grease ruins more egg whites than obviously broken yolks. Plastic bowls can hold on to grease, so use glass or stainless steel. If you're using a stand mixer that lives out on your counter, wash and thoroughly dry the bowl and whipping attachment before whipping. If so much as one speck of bacon grease wafted across the room and took roost in your mixing bowl, your egg whites won't whip.

3. Separate the eggs as soon as you take them from the refrigerator, then allow the egg whites to come to room temperature for 10 minutes or so before making meringue.

4. If the shell shatters or a small drop of yolk breaks into the whites, use a piece of shell to scoop the intruder out. The edge of the shell cuts through the white easily. If you use a spoon or your finger, you'll just chase the shell fragment around the white or blend the yolk droplet into the mix. Either way, the whites won't whip.

5. Don't tempt fate by separating all your eggs into the same bowl. Chances are the last egg you crack will spill its yolk, contaminating all your carefully separated whites. To avoid disaster, separate eggs one at a time over a small, clean bowl. Cup the cracked egg in your clean, grease-free hands and let the white slide through your fingers. If you separate the yolk intact, transfer the white to the whipping bowl. If the yolk breaks, set the egg aside and use it in an omelette, scrambled eggs, or a batch of cookies.

6. Begin by beating the egg whites on low speed until foamy.

7. If you're making meringue, add an acid to stabilize the whites. The most common acid is cream of tartar, but lemon juice also works. When the whites are foamy, add the acid and increase the speed to medium.

8. Beat the whites on medium (not high) until soft peaks form, and *then* add the sugar with the beaters running. Don't add the sugar too soon, and don't rush the process. With the beaters running, add the sugar 1 tablespoon at a time. This process can take up to 3 minutes.

9. Stop beating when the eggs are shiny and stiff. To see if the eggs are done, hold a beater upright. If the egg white keeps its shape, it's done. If it flops to one side, keep whipping.

10. Remember, more isn't always better. If you overwhip the egg whites, they'll become dull and the liquid could separate out. A copper bowl makes egg whites harder to overwhip and produces a more stable meringue. If you beat egg whites often, you might want to put "copper bowl" on your list of "Nice to Have Items."

Out of eggs? Ask a neighbor or see page 235 for substitution ideas.

Dairy

Like sugar and flour, dairy is key to the structure of baked goods. It builds the crumb, adds richness, and helps keep the texture tender. If a recipe calls for milk, water just won't do.

2% MILK: Not too rich, not too thin, this kind of milk is just right for baking. It adds tenderness, structure, and moisture to baked goods while its natural sugars aid with caramelization—something water can't do. Full-fat milk is fine to substitute, but don't use fat-free milk. It's too watery.

Milk gone sour? See page 235 for substitution ideas.

BUTTERMILK: Thick and tangy, buttermilk is, despite its name, low in fat (only 1%). It gets its name because it's a by-product of making butter, not because it contains it. Perfect for baking tender cakes, loaves, pancakes, and muffins, this slightly acid dairy product is often paired with baking soda to produce a tender result.

TIP: Buttermilk is sold almost exclusively in 1-quart containers. If you won't use it all before the expiration date, you can freeze the leftovers for up to 2 months. Thawed buttermilk is fine for baking, even though it won't be as smooth and creamy as the fresh version.

SOUR CREAM: Resist the temptation to go low-fat. You want the full 14 percent for baking. Low-fat and no-fat versions might seem like an easy way to cut fat, but they often contain thickeners, which dissolve in the heat of baking. The result will be a watery mess. In sauces, this is readily apparent. In baked goods, you'll find out after you pull the item from the oven.

HEAVY CREAM: Sometimes called whipping cream, this product has 35 percent butterfat. That's enough to turn this liquid into whipped cream—or butter if you're not careful. More than just a decadent addition, whipping cream is the only milk product that won't curdle when mixed with an acid like lemon juice or wine, and it can withstand being boiled. Substitute milk for cream with caution, because you could end up with a curdled mess.

Butter and Other Fats

Whether solid or liquid, fat plays an important role in baking. It grabs on to flavors and ensures they're delivered. It tenderizes pastries and keeps batters moist. Solid fats even help baked goods rise and make puffy, flaky pastry possible. Which should you use? That depends on what result you're after.

Butter

Butter produces a rich, tender crumb. It helps the baked good retain moisture and adds a deep flavor you can't get with shortening or vegetable oil.

Salted or unsalted?

I used to cook with salted butter. But then I noticed the bargain brand I was using was getting saltier and saltier. So I upgraded. Then I realized that the salt content varied greatly across brands—too greatly for consistent results. Unless the recipe specifically calls for salted butter, use unsalted. It's a bit more expensive but delivers more buttery flavor. The quality also tends to be better since the flavor can't hide behind a lot of salt.

That's the upside. The downside is that unsalted butter doesn't keep as long. But that doesn't stop me. I buy lots of unsalted butter when it's on sale. I leave the butter in its original foil, wrap the brick in a layer of plastic wrap, put the double-wrapped butter in a resealable freezer bag, and then pop it into the deep freeze. This works with leftover butter, as well.

What temperature?

COLD: Most scones and pastries call for cold (or even frozen) butter. The cold butter is essential to give a flaky texture. The exception—and there is always an exception—is choux pastry. (See Profiteroles on page 135.)

ROOM TEMPERATURE: The majority of cakes, cookies, and quick breads call for room temperature (also called softened) butter. Cold butter will slow down the cooking time and can make your batter grainy. But letting refrigerated butter come to room temperature on its own can take 30 to 60 minutes. And softening in the microwave is asking for trouble. Hands up if you've inadvertently melted hard butter and ended up refrigerating the mess, thus entering a potentially endless Butter Loop.

TIP: For quick room-temperature butter, give a box grater a quick squirt of cooking spray and, using the largest holes, grate the butter onto a piece of parchment or waxed paper. It will soften in about 2 minutes. To clean the grater, pour boiling water over the buttery holes and let air-dry.

MELTED: Melting butter can be done over low heat in a pot on the stove, but the easiest method is to use the microwave. I cut the butter into 1-inch pieces and then blast them on full power in 30-second bursts, checking between rounds. Because the microwave can overcook quickly, I let the last dot of butter melt on its own as I stir it in.

Measuring Butter

Some butter comes in conveniently premeasured $1/2$-cup sticks with the markings for each tablespoon on the side. It's easy to measure. If you can't find stick butter, 1-pound bricks work just as well. All you have to do is know how to measure it.

If you have a knife: Open the package. Use the edge of your knife to gently mark the midpoint. Each half is 1 cup of butter. From here, you can easily measure $\frac{1}{2}$ cup and $\frac{1}{4}$ cup. Want 1 tablespoon? Cut $\frac{1}{4}$ cup into 4 equal pieces.

If you have a scale: This is the easiest way to measure butter. All you have to remember is that 1 tablespoon of butter is $\frac{1}{2}$ ounce.

Still confused? Use the handy measurement chart on page 230.

Other Fats

SHORTENING: Shortening is made from vegetable oil. It melts more slowly than butter, which helps baked goods keep their shape. However, it has little flavor.

LARD: Ah, the classic pie dough fat. After a long, hard exile while portrayed as the artery-clogging devil of fats, lard is making a comeback. It produces the flakiest pie dough and is my mother's absolute favorite. If you like classic pies and tarts, this is the go-to ingredient.

SPREADS: They might taste like butter. They might even be made with butter, but once submitted to a process that leaves them spreadable straight from the refrigerator, they won't act like butter. Don't bake with spreads. They have too much water in them and will produce pale, tough, disappointing results. If you like spreads, put them on muffins, not in them. (Just don't tell me about it.)

OILS: Vegetable oils can create a moist and tender cake or quick bread. Grapeseed and canola are neutral-tasting oils that won't interfere with other flavors, but, depending on the recipe, olive, soybean, peanut, safflower, and sunflower oils are alternatives. Regardless of which oil you use, measure it in a measuring cup designed for liquids. Don't use a dry measure scoop.

See page 236 for substitutions for oils and butters.

Chocolate

With the rise of artisanal chocolate, many chocolate manufacturers are putting the percentage of cocoa mass on the front of their packaging. This makes it easier to pick the right chocolate. But quality can still vary widely, so once you find a chocolate you like, stick with it.

Whatever you do, avoid baking with compound chocolate. It is inferior in quality and won't deliver the desired results.

Types of Chocolate

There are many chocolate-like imitations out there. Real chocolate contains cocoa mass, sometimes called chocolate liquor, or cacao mass. That's all that's required to meet the definition. White chocolate, which contains cocoa butter but no cocoa mass, is therefore not a true chocolate. Take *that,* white chocolate.

UNSWEETENED OR BITTER CHOCOLATE: This dark chocolate contains cocoa mass and cocoa butter—no sugar. It's often used in cakes and brownies to deliver intense chocolate flavor.

BITTERSWEET OR SEMISWEET CHOCOLATE: Technically, there is a slight difference between these two dark chocolates, but the percentage of cocoa mass isn't regulated, so it can vary. For the recipes in this book, bittersweet and semisweet chocolate can be used interchangeably. Let your taste guide you. Most supermarkets stock only semisweet in the baking section, so don't fuss if the recipe specifies bittersweet.

MILK CHOCOLATE: With as little as 10 percent cocoa mass and lots of cocoa butter and milk solids, this is a mild, creamy chocolate. The stuff of Easter bunnies and children's candies, it tends to be quite sweet. It also burns easily, so if you are melting it, keep an eye on the process.

WHITE CHOCOLATE: While this is technically not real chocolate, it is often used like it—as chips and for coating or drizzles. It has a sweet taste that won't compete with delicate flavors that dark chocolate can overpower. Visually, it provides a striking contrast to dark and milk chocolate.

CHOCOLATE CHIPS: Whether they are semisweet, milk, or white, chocolate chips are designed to keep their shape when you bake with them. If a recipe calls for chocolate chips that are just stirred into the batter and not melted, then you can use semisweet, milk, or white chocolate, according to

TIP: Don't let the flexible nature of chocolate chips lull you into a false sense of chocolate security. Swapping baking chocolate for chips in this cavalier manner will alter your recipes, sometimes with disastrous results. See the substitution chart on page 236 before you go swapping baking chocolate.

your taste. I always use semisweet chips, especially when white are called for. I have a friend who does the opposite. We rarely fight over cookies.

Storage: Store wrapped chocolate in a cool, dry place for up to 6 months. Yes, only 6 months. Some of mine is reaching the expiration date. Better use it up.

What's the white film?

It's called bloom. It doesn't affect how the chocolate tastes or bakes, but it does tell you that you've stored it at too high a temperature. If your chocolate consistently has a bloom, it's a sign you need to find a cooler storage spot.

Cocoa

COCOA POWDER: This is cocoa mass in powdered form. Without cocoa butter, it provides an intense chocolate taste without a lot of fat. Sometimes called natural cocoa, it's slightly acidic. It has a fruitier taste than Dutch-process cocoa. Recipes calling for natural cocoa usually call for baking soda to neutralize the acidity. Most supermarket brands of cocoa powder fall into this category.

DUTCH-PROCESS COCOA: This cocoa has been specially treated to reduce the acidity and has a neutral pH. As a result, it's darker, richer, and less bitter than the standard cocoa powder. It's often paired with baking powder in recipes. If you're dusting chocolate truffles with plain cocoa, Dutch-process is the best choice, because it's less bitter yet intense. See page 236 for information on substituting cocoa powders.

INSTANT COCOA POWDER: This is a presweetened mix for making hot chocolate. Don't confuse it with cocoa powder. If you have it in your cupboard, add hot milk, top with marshmallows, and sip while reading the recipes. Just don't bake with it.

Storage: Unlike chocolate, cocoa powder keeps almost indefinitely. Mine never lasts long enough to test this theory. Store it in a cool, dry place, away from moisture. Don't refrigerate or freeze it.

How to Melt Chocolate

Chocolate can be fussy. It throws a hissy fit if exposed to water of any temperature. The technical term for this is *seize*. Because of its water aversion, never cover chocolate while melting. The condensation on the lid can drip onto the chocolate and cause it to seize (lump up and become grainy).

Chocolate needs to be melted gently and with indirect heat. You can't toss it into a hot pan because it scorches easily—and once it does, there's no salvaging it. If the recipe calls for cream or butter, you can sometimes melt them along with the chocolate and further reduce the chance of scorching.

Here are two easy methods to melt chocolate. Note that no matter which method you use, milk chocolate and white chocolate take less time to melt than dark and are more prone to burning.

Before you begin to melt the chocolate, always break or chop the chocolate into small pieces. Aim for the size of jumbo chocolate chips. This helps the chocolate melt more quickly and evenly. If you place a big piece of chocolate in a pot, it will melt eventually; but if you're like me, you'll run out of patience, crank up the heat, and ruin everything by burning it.

Stove-top method: Place a double boiler or heatproof bowl over a pot of hot, not boiling, water. The bottom of the bowl should not touch the water. (If the water boils, steam can escape and splatter your chocolate.) As the chocolate begins to melt, give it a gentle stir. When the chocolate is almost melted, remove it from the heat and stir to dissolve the last few stubborn pieces.

Microwave method: Every microwave is different. To ensure you don't burn the chocolate, melt small pieces in a microwaveable bowl with your microwave oven's power level set to high for dark and 50 percent for milk or white. Zap it in 60-second bursts, checking the progress and giving it a stir in between. When the chocolate is slightly melted, continue zapping at 30-second bursts. When most of the chocolate is melted, remove the bowl and stir until the last few stubborn bits have melted. If they refuse, return it to the microwave for 15 more seconds at reduced power. Continue to zap and stir until the chocolate is smooth.

How to Drizzle Chocolate

Chocolate is the perfect edible paint. Grab an offset spatula and layer it on like Cézanne. Channel your inner Jackson Pollock and let it drip free-form on your ~~canvas~~ cake. When you're done, you can even sign your name. All you need is some melted chocolate and a little artistic inspiration.

SPOON TECHNIQUE

This low-tech approach requires nothing but a spoon. Simply dip it in the melted chocolate, pass it gently back and forth over your baked goods, and let the chocolate fall where it may. When you're done, lick the spoon.

PLASTIC BAG TECHNIQUE

This requires almost no cleanup. Just pour the melted chocolate into a sandwich bag or freezer bag. If you have access to Canadian milk bags, clean ones are excellent for piping. Press all the chocolate to one corner, snip a small hole in the corner of the bag, and play.

PARCHMENT PAPER CONE

Don't like to send plastic to the landfill? Then make an environmentally friendly version of a piping bag using biodegradable, compostable parchment paper to drizzle your chocolate.

Some fairly easy tasks sound complicated when you describe them in words—like tying your shoe or buttoning a shirt. Making a paper cone is one of those things. Sure, it has a fancy French name, *cornet* (kor-NAY), but it's just a paper cone dressed up to show off. While it's easy to make and adds less than a minute to the drizzling task, it does involve an isosceles triangle. Don't panic, there's no calculus required.

1. Cut a square of parchment—about 10 inches wide.

2. Cut the square in half diagonally so you have an isosceles triangle. (In this case, the short sides are the same length.)

3. Place the triangle on the counter in front of you with the long side nearest you. Use one finger to hold down the point farthest from you.

4. Grab the right corner and roll it up and inward until it touches the point your finger is holding. Line up the points. This is the first half of your cornet.

5. Grab the left corner and wrap it over the cone you're forming and tuck it underneath to bring its corner to meet the other two from behind. All three corners should now meet, and the cone should form such a tight tip, you can't see through it. If not, slide the corners around until the cone is tight. Once you have the shape you want, fold the three tips over twice toward the inside of the cone to secure things.

6. Fill the cone with the melted chocolate (or frosting—did I mention this works with frosting?). Then close the top, fold the corners toward the center, and fold the top down to seal the cone. Roll the top toward the filling like it's a toothpaste tube.

7. Using scissors, snip a tiny bit off the tip of the cone. Go smaller than you think you should. Chocolate doesn't need much of an opening. You can always make the opening bigger, but you can't make it smaller.

8. Drizzle the chocolate. Write words. Make stars. Doodle.

You can use this trick with piping tips, too. Start with a bigger parchment triangle and snip a bigger hole to hold the piping tip. This works for large piping jobs like profiteroles (page 135).

Use any of these drizzle techniques to decorate biscotti (page 112), Florentines (page 176), or even palmiers (page 64).

Nuts

Toasting brings out the flavor of nuts and adds crispness. If a recipe calls for toasted nuts and you choose to skip this step, the baked good won't be as crunchy or as flavorful.

When toasting, rely on your eyes and nose more than timing. You want the nuts to begin to brown and smell fragrant but not be fully toasted, as they will continue to cook once removed from the heat. Stop toasting them just before you think they're done. If you don't remove them in time, you can help halt the cooking process by transferring them to a cold platter.

Microwave method: This method requires your attention. It's my least favorite method because every microwave works differently and predicting the timing is impossible. My old clunker of a microwave is slow and rarely overcooks nuts. My mother-in-law's new one burns them in half the time.

In general, toasting nuts in a microwave takes 5 to 7 minutes. Place the nuts in a single layer on a microwaveable plate and cook in 1-minute intervals, stirring in between. When the nuts begin to smell fragrant, reduce to 30-second increments since they can burn easily. Stop when the nuts are very fragrant and warm to the touch. Let cool before using.

TIP: Hazelnuts need to have their bitter skins removed. Once you've toasted them, place them on a clean kitchen towel and rub them to remove the skins. You won't get all the skins off, but as long as you get more than half, the recipe should turn out just fine.

Oven method: Place nuts in a single layer on a rimmed baking pan. Bake in a preheated 350°F oven for 7 to 15 minutes, or until the nuts start to become fragrant, stirring occasionally to help them toast evenly. Because different nuts toast at different rates, keep an eye, nose, and hand on them. Remove the nuts from the oven when they smell very fragrant and are warm, not scorching hot, to the touch, and then let cool. This is my method of choice when I have the oven already preheating.

Pan method: If you won't be turning on the oven, you can toast nuts in a dry frying pan. A nonstick pan works well. Toast the nuts over medium heat, stirring often, until they begin to brown and smell fragrant. This technique is faster than the oven method but can burn the nuts more quickly. Don't leave the stove.

Storage

Because of their high fat content, nuts can go rancid. To extend their shelf life, store nuts in the refrigerator or freezer. Refrigerated nuts last a few months. Frozen, they can last up to a year. Not sure if they're okay? Taste them. You'll know.

Nut substitutions

In baking, nuts are usually a matter of personal taste. While some flavor combinations are classic (cherries with almonds), you can usually substitute nuts to suit your taste without consequences. Popular baking nuts include walnuts, pecans, almonds, hazelnuts, pistachios, pine nuts, Brazil nuts, macadamia nuts, and cashews. Even peanuts, which are technically legumes, can be swapped in.

Flavor Enhancers

Even vanilla needs butter or salt to shine. The items in this section add flavor to baked goods. Here's how to use them to show them off best.

Citrus

Lemon, lime, and orange peel add lovely flavor to baked goods, sauces, and even salad dressings.

PEEL: The peel, or zest, is the thin, colorful outer layer but not the whole rind: The white part is the pith, and it's bitter. Before zesting citrus, wash the fruit to remove dirt and germs. Then use a microplane or the fine holes of a box grater to remove only the

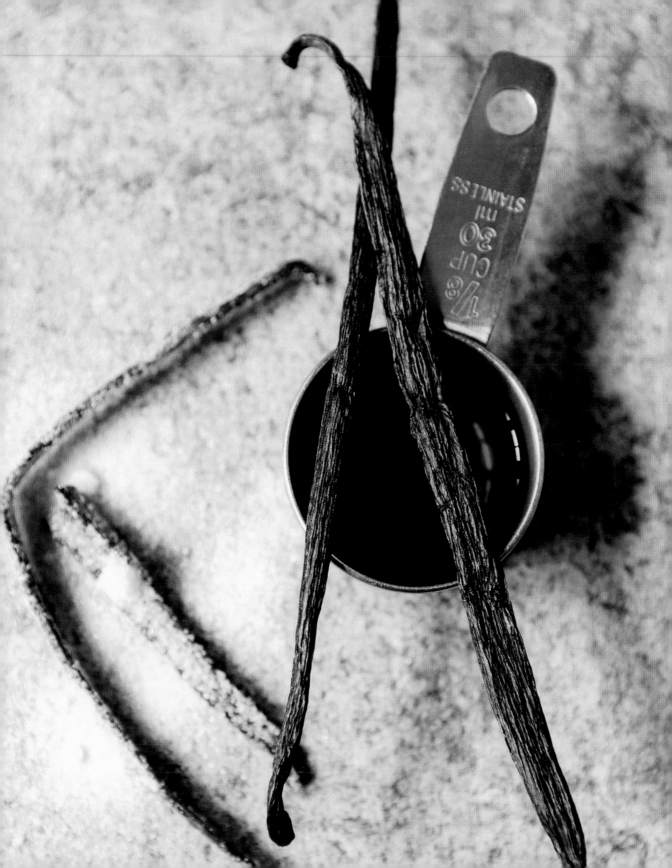

colored portion of the rind. The finer the grater, the more oils get released, and with them more flavor.

For accuracy, grate the fruit over waxed or parchment paper and then use the paper to funnel the peel into the measuring spoon. Scooping can compact the peel and provide inaccurate measurements. I usually like more peel than less, but sometimes subtlety is required.

JUICE: If possible, always use freshly squeezed lemon or lime juice in baking. The bottled kind can leave an unpleasant metallic taste, especially if used in large quantities. Commercial orange juice, on the other hand, bakes quite nicely.

Coffee

COFFEE: When is coffee not coffee? When it's used as a chocolate enhancer. Some chocolate recipes use brewed or instant coffee to deepen the chocolate taste rather than create mocha. Don't tell coffee haters if you use this trick. They might not even notice.

ESPRESSO POWDER: Sometimes you want the intensity of espresso but not the added liquid. Espresso powder is the answer because it dissolves completely while delivering the taste. You can buy high-end espresso packets at high-end coffee shops or find less expensive versions on your grocery store shelves. Regular instant coffee isn't quite the same but will do in a pinch if you increase the amount used. Be warned, though: Too much standard instant coffee can leave a metallic taste. Don't use ground espresso, even if it's finely ground. It won't dissolve and will make your baked good feel like it's full of grit.

Herbs and Spices

HERBS: Most herbs deliver more flavor when they're fresh. If you don't have fresh herbs on hand, the rule of thumb is 1 tablespoon fresh herb = 1 teaspoon dried. Store dried herbs in a cool, dry place, and replace them every 6 months or so for optimum freshness. Buying small quantities in bulk is a great way to ensure your herbs are always full of flavor.

TIP: Many hard spices work best when freshly grated or ground. A microplane ensures you have freshly ground nutmeg and cinnamon on command. If you like to grind your own Indian spices, use a mortar and pestle or coffee grinder devoted to spices only. Mine is clearly labeled "FOR SPICES ONLY!!!" Each exclamation mark is earned. Three guesses why.

SPICES: Old Spice might be a popular aftershave, but old spices won't win anyone over in the kitchen. Even if they look fine, outdated spices can lose their flavor. I once used a package of dried chiles that had been around for oh, I don't know, forever. They had gotten lost in the back of the cupboard, and I didn't want to "waste" them. Big mistake. My bean soup took a heaping tablespoon and was barely warm. So did the pot of chili and the pasta sauce. When I replaced the package with fresh dried chiles and applied the old measurements, I nearly died of heat.

Salt

In baking, salt often goes unnoticed, but it plays a crucial role. It intensifies and brightens flavors, brings spices into balance, and keeps yeast in check. Although you might not taste the salt, without it, baked goods can taste flat, like there's something missing. And that something would be salt.

How much salt it takes to strike the right balance is a matter of taste. The only exception to the salt-as-you-please rule is with yeasted breads. Here, the salt actually controls the yeast's growth. Without it, the bread would rise rapidly. A slow rise helps develop not only the flavor but also the texture. Don't skip the salt in yeasted recipes. Other than that? Let your palate decide.

Baking Salt

FINE SEA SALT: I use this for most of my baking. It dissolves easily and contains no anti-clumping chemicals. Once hard to find, fine sea salt is now available at the grocery store and can be relatively inexpensive. You don't have to get fancy with this sea salt. Save your money for chocolate.

Finishing Salt

This type of salt goes on baked goods either after they emerge from the oven or just as they are going in. You can spend a lot of money on high-end finishing salts, so don't put them in your baking. They'd just be wasted.

COARSE SEA SALT: This adds a lovely flavor and texture to recipes but is too coarse to dissolve into the batter like fine sea salt. Use it at the table or just before popping baked goods into the oven.

FLEUR DE SEL: Maldon is the best known and easiest to find fleur de sel. It's flaky and versatile, perfect for toppings where you want a hit of salt to play against the sweet or to bring out flavors without overpowering.

KOSHER SALT: Coarser and lighter than table salt, kosher salt is also less salty. It's not often used in baking, but can be sprinkled on focaccia and pizza for an attractive, not-so-salty topping.

Vanilla

If I didn't know what a vanilla pod looked like and I came upon one lying on the counter, I'd bludgeon it with my shoe. How can one of the most wonderful flavors on Earth be housed in a casing that resembles a leathery, black eel? While the vanilla flower is exquisite, the bean that renders the most important baking essence in the world is butt ugly.

And expensive.

Vanilla beans start at about $3 each and go up. But despite their off-putting looks and high price tag, nothing, *nothing* tastes like real vanilla.

Forms of Vanilla

Vanilla is one of my favorite flavors. I can't imagine baking without it. I went through two large bottles of Mexican vanilla developing this book. That doesn't include all the pods, the paste, and the vanilla sugar.

Vanilla is added to many cakes and cookies even when other stronger flavors are present. Why? Vanilla tones down butter, smooths chocolate's rough edges, and enriches almost any sweet.

Whole Beans

Long, thin, leathery, and supple, a vanilla bean doesn't look like something you'd want to put in your cupcakes. And it isn't. At least not whole. Split the bean open. The inside is full of tiny black seeds called vanilla caviar.

USE THEM FOR: Beguiling as the caviar is, the flavor is mainly in the pod. Use the whole bean in recipes where you can steep it in a liquid (such as the crème anglaise on page 222). The caviar can be added to the liquid, providing the tiny black flecks that say to the eater, "I was made with real vanilla beans." Once steeped, don't discard the pods. Recycle them into sugar (page 39).

Vanilla Extract

When you buy extract, look for the bottle that says "pure." "Flavoring" is code for "fake."

USE IT FOR: baked goods where the alcohol can evaporate

Double and Triple Vanilla Extract

This is like vanilla extract only more so. As the name indicates, these specialty vanillas are stronger than the standard. You can use half or a third to obtain the same amount of flavor, but I like to use the amount called for in the recipe for two to three times the flavor without extra liquid.

USE IT FOR: more flavor in baked goods and icings where you want more intense vanilla without adding more liquid

Vanilla Bean Paste

This dark brown paste is bursting with vanilla seeds and delivers wonderful vanilla flavor without requiring you to scrape or steep the pod. You can use it in place of vanilla extract if you run out. This thick paste used to be available only in specialty shops, but I've started to see it in some large supermarkets. A lot depends on demand, so if you like vanilla paste, tell the store manager, who just might stock it for you.

USE IT FOR: a substitution for vanilla beans

Store vanilla beans, extract, or paste in a cool, dry place. The whole beans can be kept in the tube they came in—again, in a cupboard away from moisture. Don't store them in the refrigerator.

All things being equal: 1 vanilla bean (split and scraped) = 1 tablespoon pure vanilla extract = 1 tablespoon vanilla bean paste

Vanilla Varieties

There's no such thing as plain old vanilla. The bean with the caviar also has *terroir*. Depending on where the bean is grown and how it's processed, vanilla delivers markedly different flavors. There are at least half a dozen different vanillas, but only three are found commonly in our supermarkets and specialty shops.

TAHITIAN: Fruity and floral, this goes well with fruit and custards.

MADAGASCAR: Also called Madagascar Bourbon, this is the most common vanilla and plays nicely with all baked goods.

MEXICAN: This is my absolute favorite. It's straightforward, clean, and well balanced with just a tiny hint of spice. I could drink it.

Vanilla Sugar

Vanilla sugar is where steeped and scraped pods go to die.

VANILLA SUGAR—THE SLOW WAY

You can make as much as you want with this ratio. Use it in place of granulated sugar in baked goods to boost the flavor. For a garnish, infuse turbinado sugar.

1. Split the vanilla bean lengthwise. Place in a jar with a tight-fitting lid.

2. Pour the sugar over the bean pieces, tighten the lid, and give it a shake or two to distribute the sugar and bury the beans.

3. Place in a cool, dry place for a week or two.

4. Replenish as needed with more beans and sugar.

1 vanilla bean (whole or with the caviar removed)

2 cups granulated sugar

INSTANT VANILLA SUGAR

If you want vanilla sugar and you want it now, you can have it. This quick-dissolving vanilla-flavored powdered sugar is ideal for coffee, tea, hot chocolate, whipped cream, and anywhere you want a spoonful of flavor to disappear into the mix.

1. Cut the bean into 3 or 4 pieces.

2. Place the bean pieces and sugar in a blender and pulse until the bean is fully incorporated. The results will be a slightly beige powder.

3. Store in an airtight jar.

1 vanilla bean (whole or with the caviar removed)

2 cups granulated sugar

PASTRY

It seems you either find the phrase "easy as pie" fitting or throw your flour-dusted hands in the air and pull out the premade store brand. The recipes in this section were tested by people who weren't confident in their pastry-making skills. They are now.

If you already have trusted pastry recipes in your repertoire, go ahead and use them. If you don't, here are some recipes that work and tips on how to use them.

DEMYSTIFYING PASTRY

To hear some people talk, you'd think pastry was the prima donna of the baking world. I've heard it described as moody, difficult, and even a witch to work with. In reality, it's more like a scared child. It likes things a certain way, and as long as you know its needs, you can coax it into playing nicely—almost every time.

Sometimes Heat Is the Enemy

Baking a pie on a hot day won't just strain your air conditioner; it can actually cause issues with your pastry. Pie dough just doesn't like a hot environment. If possible, schedule summer baking for early morning or later at night. And make sure the fat you use is cold. If your kitchen is warm and you must bake, chill the bowl to give your dough a fighting chance. If you're lucky enough to have granite countertops or a marble board, cool the work surface with ice cubes placed in a resealable bag before rolling the dough.

Measure Twice, Blend Once

Professional chefs measure by weight for accuracy, but millions of home cooks have been making successful pastry for generations using nothing more than measuring cups and hard-earned experience. For accuracy, spoon flour into a dry measure and level it off with a knife. Scooping compacts the flour and can make your dough tough.

Cut the Fat—Literally

Whether you use a food processor, a pastry blender, or two knives, the key to flaky, tender pastry is to cut in cold fat until it is about the size of small peas—not coarse crumbs, as some recipes suggest. If your recipe uses butter, a box grater takes the guesswork out (see page 25).

Handle the Dough

Unlike the flour, the amount of moisture you add is not precise. You'll have to rely on feel. The dough needs enough water so it holds together when pressed between your fingers but not so much that it forms a ball. Too much water makes pastry tough. If your recipe suggests a range of measurements, use the smallest amount and add more until you reach the right consistency. Use ice-cold water and sprinkle it over the flour-fat mixture so it distributes evenly. Don't dump it in one spot.

Chill Out

It's often hard to wait, but pie dough should be chilled for at least an hour before rolling. Not only does this relax the gluten in the wheat, making it more tender, it makes the dough easier to handle. Just form the dough into a disk, wrap it in plastic wrap, and pop it in the fridge. You can refrigerate premade dough for up to 3 days or freeze it for a couple of months.

Ready to Roll

Before rolling chilled dough, be sure to let it warm up; otherwise, it will crack. But don't let it get too warm or it will stick. The dough is ready to roll when your finger can make an indentation without going all the way through. If your finger sinks to the counter, the dough is too warm. If it barely dents the surface, it's too cold.

When your dough is ready to roll, roll it on a floured pastry board or pastry cloth. Roll from the center out, being careful not to work too much extra flour into the dough. Once your dough is transferred to the pie or tart tins, chill it again—this time just for 15 minutes. This will keep the pastry from shrinking.

Sometimes Heat Is Your Friend

Once you're ready to bake, heat is crucial. Make sure your oven has been preheated for at least 20 minutes. This helps ensure a more stable heat when you open the oven door.

Nice but Not Necessary

Place your pie on a baking sheet. This catches drips and helps create a crisper bottom crust. Feeling confident, now? Here are some recipes.

CHEATER'S PUFF PASTRY

True puff pastry is a major commitment requiring several rollings with long waits in between. In some ways, it's easier to raise children. They eventually grow up and ignore you. But genuine puff pastry is like a newborn, demanding your full attention every half hour.

This version is a bit of work but hardly more than standard pastry. Although it isn't quite as flaky as traditional puff pastry, I use it for sweet palmiers (page 64) and savory tarts (pages 57 and 58). No one has ever noticed it's not the real deal.

MAKES FOUR 10" × 10" SHEETS | COMMITMENT LEVEL: DONE IN STAGES

3½ cups all-purpose flour

1¾ teaspoons fine sea salt

1 pound (2 cups) cold unsalted butter

1 cup cold water

NOTE: The dough can be refrigerated for up to 4 days or frozen in an airtight freezer bag for up to 2 weeks. Each of the four rectangles is approximately the quantity of a commercial package of puff pastry.

1. In the large bowl of a food processor fitted with a steel blade, combine the flour and salt with a few pulses.

2. Cut the butter into ½" cubes. Add ¼ cup of the cubed butter to the flour mixture and pulse until you can't see pieces of butter. This takes about ten 2-second pulses. Add the rest of the butter and pulse a few times until the butter is the size of peas. You might have to remove the lid after a few pulses and stir the flour up from the bottom.

3. With the lid removed, pour the water evenly over the flour mixture. Don't dump it in one spot. Pulse a few times until the dough looks rough. Stop before the mixture comes together.

4. Turn the crumbly dough onto a piece of floured waxed paper. Using floured hands, press the dough into a square. Dust the dough lightly with flour, top with waxed paper, and roll the dough, occasionally turning it 90 degrees, until you have an 18" square.

5. Cut the square in half down the length of the waxed paper. Roll 1 piece of dough into a 12" × 18" rectangle. Using the bottom sheet of waxed paper, fold the dough in thirds along the long edge, creating a 4" × 18" strip. From the short end, roll the dough up tightly. Press the roll with your palms to make a rough rectangle, about 6" × 4". Repeat with the other piece of dough. You may need a clean sheet of waxed paper.

6. Cut each rectangle in half. You now have 4 pieces of dough. Wrap each in plastic wrap and refrigerate for at least 1 hour. Bake according to recipe directions.

NO-FAIL PASTRY THREE WAYS

No-fail pastry delivers excellent results consistently. The egg, lemon juice or vinegar, and ice-cold water are key. But which fat to use? My mom loves the shattery, crisp-flaky crust only lard can deliver. My father is perfectly happy with a shorter, more crumbly shortening crust. Me? I love the rich butter version. Regardless of which fat you choose, I've got you covered.

NO-FAIL PASTRY (LARD OR SHORTENING VERSION)

The key is very cold fat and not overhandling. These pastries are perfect for pies, galettes, and tarts.

MAKES ENOUGH FOR 2 SINGLE PIE CRUSTS, 1 DOUBLE-CRUST PIE, OR LOTS OF TARTS | COMMITMENT LEVEL: DONE IN STAGES

1. In a large bowl, mix the flour and salt. Using a pastry blender or 2 knives, cut in the lard or shortening until it is about the size of small peas. (A few regular pea-size pieces are fine.)

2. In a small bowl, beat together the egg yolk, 4 tablespoons of ice water, and the vinegar or lemon juice with a fork. Pour over the flour mixture and mix with the fork. If more water is needed, add up to 2 tablespoons, one at a time. The dough will be ragged but should hold together when squeezed between your fingers. Turn the dough onto a lightly floured surface and knead briefly until the dough holds together. Don't overhandle.

3. Divide the dough in half and shape each piece into a disk. Wrap in plastic wrap or place in a resealable plastic bag. Refrigerate for 1 hour. If you chill the dough longer, you might have to let it sit on the counter for a few minutes to soften before rolling. Roll and bake according to recipe directions.

NOTE: The dough can be refrigerated for up to 3 days or frozen for up to 3 months.

2½ cups all-purpose flour

¾ teaspoon fine sea salt

1 cup very cold lard or shortening, cut into cubes

1 egg yolk

4 tablespoons ice water, plus up to 2 tablespoons more if needed

1 tablespoon white vinegar or fresh lemon juice

NO-FAIL PASTRY (BUTTER VERSION)

Getting the fat cut into this pastry evenly is often the biggest challenge when making this recipe. Grating in frozen butter is an easy fix that delivers consistent results. Butter produces a lovely, tender pie crust that melts in your mouth. It won't shatter like lard, but it has a delicate quality all its own.

MAKES ENOUGH FOR 2 SINGLE PIE CRUSTS, 1 DOUBLE-CRUST PIE, OR LOTS OF TARTS |
COMMITMENT LEVEL: DONE IN STAGES

¾ cup very cold unsalted butter

2½ cups all-purpose flour

½ teaspoon fine sea salt

1 egg yolk

1 tablespoon fresh lemon juice or white vinegar

4–6 tablespoons ice water

> **TIP:** If you're baking a pie or tarts and want a slightly sweeter pastry, you can add 1 tablespoon of granulated sugar to the flour when you sift it with the salt.

1. About 15 minutes before you begin making the pastry, pop the cold butter into the freezer.

2. Into a large bowl, sift the flour and salt. Using the large holes of a box grater, grate the frozen butter over the flour mixture. Toss to combine.

3. In a small bowl, whisk the egg yolk, lemon juice or vinegar, and 4 tablespoons of the ice water. Pour over the flour mixture and stir, adding more ice water as needed. The dough should be a bit ragged but will hold together when squeezed in your fingers.

4. Turn the dough out onto a lightly floured surface and knead briefly. Divide the dough in half and shape each piece into a disk. Wrap each disk in plastic wrap or place in a resealable plastic bag. Refrigerate for at least 1 hour. Allow the dough to sit on the counter for a few minutes before rolling. Roll and bake according to recipe directions.

NOTE: The dough can be refrigerated for up to 3 days or frozen for up to 3 months.

PÂTE SUCRÉE

Don't think of this as pastry. Think of it as shortbread in a pie pan. Notoriously messy, this recipe demands you get your fingers dirty.

MAKES ENOUGH FOR A 10" PIE | COMMITMENT LEVEL: DONE IN STAGES

1¼ cups all-purpose flour

⅔ cup sifted confectioners' sugar

¼ teaspoon fine sea salt

½ cup cold unsalted butter, cut into small pieces

2 eggs, lightly beaten at room temperature

1 teaspoon pure vanilla extract

1. In the bowl of a food processor fitted with a steel blade, combine the flour, confectioners' sugar, and salt with a few pulses. Add the butter and pulse in 2-second bursts until the pieces are the size of peas. Lightly whisk the eggs with the vanilla and pour evenly over the flour mixture. Pulse a few times. The dough will be crumbly but will hold together if you squeeze it.

2. Dust your hands in flour and press the dough into a 10" tart pan.

3. Chill for at least 30 minutes before baking according to recipe directions.

NOTE: The dough can be kept well wrapped in the refrigerator for several days or frozen for up to 3 months.

WORKING WITH PHYLLO PASTRY

Phyllo is the shattery pastry found wrapped around many Greek and Middle Eastern treats. Thin as tissue paper, it's notoriously hard to make from scratch. While I occasionally make my own puff pastry (see page 44), I always buy phyllo. And I don't care who knows it.

Phyllo usually comes in 1-pound packages and can be found in the freezer section of any major grocery store. Sheets come in different sizes, the most common being 14″ × 9″, 18″ × 12″, or 18″ × 14″. I used 18″ × 12″ sheets for the baking in this book. All rolling instructions are based on these dimensions. Even if your phyllo sheets are off by an inch or so, don't worry. These are general guidelines. If you look inside the phyllo box, you will see a wide range of rolling options printed on the inside. There is no one way. The best system is the one that works for you.

The following works for me.

BEFORE YOU BEGIN

While all that phyllo is a challenge to make by hand, it's relatively easy to work with—as long as you don't let the sheets dry out or work with it before it's fully defrosted. A word of warning: You can't rush the process by trying to defrost phyllo in the microwave. Believe me. I tried and ended up making an unscheduled trip back to the store. For phyllo success:

1. Defrost the phyllo according to the package directions.

2. Once the phyllo is ready to use, unwrap and place on a flat surface.

3. Place a clean, damp tea towel on the stack of phyllo sheets to prevent them from drying out and cracking. *Damp* is the operative word. Too wet and you'll have a different problem on your hands.

4. Remove a sheet of phyllo. Return the tea towel to the stack. Be diligent. It takes only a few minutes for the dough to dry out. Once dry, phyllo shatters and is impossible to work with.

TIP: Most recipes instruct you to brush the phyllo with melted butter. I use a neutral oil instead. Why? Oil is less of a hassle. I never melt enough butter. Or I melt too much. If I'm folding a lot of pieces, the water in melted butter tends to separate, and the rapidly coagulating butter clogs my pastry brush. While butter does add flavor, the filling is usually tasty enough to make up for using oil. The instructions in the book call for oil, but you can always use melted butter if you prefer.

TRIANGLES: APPETIZER SIZE

1. Cut the stack of phyllo sheets in half across the long side. You want sheets approximately 9″ × 12″. Stack the phyllo sheets on top of each other, remove one sheet, and place the damp towel on top of the phyllo stack.

2. Brush the sheet lightly with oil. Fold the sheet in thirds lengthwise so you have a long, thin strip (3″ × 12″ inches) three layers thick.

3. Place 1 tablespoon of filling at the bottom of the sheet toward the left side.

4. Fold the bottom right corner up over the filling to touch the left edge. This forms a triangle. Maintaining the triangle shape, continue rolling the phyllo up the strip.

5. Place the triangle seam side down on a baking sheet. Brush the top with more oil. Bake according to the recipe directions.

TRIANGLES: SINGLE-SERVING SIZE

1. Remove one sheet from under the damp towel and lightly brush with oil.

2. Fold the phyllo sheet in thirds by bringing the short sides toward the middle to make one long strip (6″ × 12″ inches) three layers thick.

3. Place $\frac{1}{4}$ cup filling at the bottom toward the left side, about $\frac{1}{2}$″ from the bottom edge.

4. Fold the bottom right corner up over the filling to touch the left edge. This forms a triangle. Maintaining the triangle shape, continue rolling the phyllo up the strip.

5. Place the triangle seam side down on a baking sheet. Brush with more oil and bake according to the recipe directions.

ROLLS: APPETIZER SIZE

1. Cut the stack of phyllo sheets in half across the long side. You want sheets approximately 9″ × 12″. Stack the phyllo sheets on top of each other, remove one sheet, and place the damp towel on top of the phyllo stack.

2. Place the phyllo sheet on the counter with the short side toward you. Brush the sheet with oil.

3. Place 1 tablespoon of filling in the center, about $\frac{1}{2}$″ from the bottom edge. Roll the phyllo over the filling toward the top of the sheet, until you are about halfway up the sheet.

4. Fold the side edges over the filling, toward the center. You'll have a roll about 3″ wide. Finish rolling the bundle.

5. Place seam side down on a baking sheet. Brush the top with more oil. Bake according to the recipe directions.

ROLLS: SINGLE-SERVING SIZE

1. Remove one sheet from under the damp towel and lightly brush with oil.

2. Fold the phyllo sheet in thirds by bringing the short sides toward the middle to make one long strip (about 6″ × 12″) three layers thick.

3. Place ¼ cup filling at the bottom in the center, about ½" from the bottom edge. Roll the phyllo over the filling toward the top of the sheet, until you are about halfway up the sheet.

4. Fold the side edges over the filling, toward the center. Finish rolling the bundle.

5. Place seam side down on the baking sheet. Brush with more oil and bake according to the recipe directions.

MUFFIN CUP BUNDLES

These are the ultimate cheat. No rolling, wrapping, or fiddling.

1. Brush a sheet of phyllo with oil. Place a second sheet on top of the first and brush it again. Repeat until you have three oiled sheets stacked on top of each other.

2. Using a sharp knife, cut the phyllo into six 6" squares (3" across and 2" down).

3. Place a square over the cup of a 12-cup muffin pan. Gently press it into the cup, being careful not to tear the pastry. You can use your knuckles, the back of an ice cream scoop, or a small ladle.

4. Place ¼ cup of filling into the cup; fold the corners over the filling. Brush with more oil. Bake according to the recipe directions.

FLAKY

foods that shatter when bitten into

Pastry is like snowflakes—no two shattered bits are alike. Bite into a palmier, slice a tart, or break open a samosa and flakes will flutter to the table like ice crystals falling from the sky. You never know where they will land. Some fall straight and true in a neat pile on the plate below. Some waft about in an unfelt breeze drifting so far from your fork, you wonder how they got there.

Flour, butter, and heat make flakes possible. Consider them proof of a job well done.

FLAKY

SAVORY

SWEET

MUSHROOM, LEEK, AND GRUYÈRE TART

If vegetables were looking to elect a spokesperson, I'd nominate mushrooms. A bit of heat brings out the best in them. And when things get downright hot, they maintain their composure, refusing to dissolve into an incoherent mash. They work graciously with almost any herb, are effusively complementary to dairy, and are as comfortable with fancy-dress pastry as they are with a Casual Friday slice of toast. With a support staff of herbs, cheese, and garlic, this recipe lets the earthiness of mushrooms shine.

MAKES 4 TO 6 SERVINGS | COMMITMENT LEVEL: READY IN AN HOUR OR LESS

1. Preheat the oven to 425°F.

2. On a sheet of parchment paper cut to fit a rimmed baking sheet, roll the puff pastry sheet out to a 10″ square. Using a sharp knife, gently score the pastry an inch inside the outer edge, being careful not to cut all the way through. Place the parchment with the scored pastry onto a rimmed baking sheet. Refrigerate while you prepare the filling.

3. In a large skillet over medium heat, melt the butter. When it bubbles, grate the garlic on a microplane into the pan. Add the thyme. Cook gently for 1 minute. Add the leeks and cook until they begin to soften. Add the mushrooms and cook until they are soft but not weeping juices. Place the mushroom filling into a strainer and let drain for a few minutes.

4. Spoon the mushroom filling onto the pastry, being careful to keep inside the score marks. Add a grinding of fresh black pepper, if using. Bake for 15 minutes. Remove the tart from the oven and sprinkle with the cheese. Bake for 5 minutes, or until the cheese has melted and the pastry is golden brown. Serve while hot.

NOTE: This tart is best eaten as soon as it is cool enough to handle. Leftovers can be wrapped and refrigerated, but the pastry will suffer. To reheat, pop under the broiler for a few minutes. Do not reheat in the microwave.

1 sheet commercial puff pastry or homemade Cheater's Puff Pastry (page 44), defrosted

3 tablespoons unsalted butter

2 cloves garlic

2 sprigs fresh thyme, leaves only (see tip)

2 cups thinly sliced leeks, white parts only, sliced lengthwise and slivered into half moons

16 ounces cremini or portobello mushrooms, cut into 1″ pieces

Ground black pepper (optional)

3 ounces grated Gruyère cheese

TIP: To strip the thyme leaves from the stem in seconds, simply grasp the top of the sprig between your thumb and index finger. Using your other hand, gently pull the stem through your pinched fingers. The leaves will strip right off, no chopping required. This also works for rosemary, although you might want to mince the rosemary leaves, depending on the use.

ROASTED BUTTERNUT SQUASH AND SAGE TART

Would a squash by any other name taste as sweet? Quite likely, especially if you roasted it. Roasting brings out the best in squash, as well as its natural sugars. It leaves the vegetable tender on the inside yet creates a bit of exterior texture when you bite. Add some sage, which I suspect was created specifically with roasted squash in mind, and you have a dish that's poetry in a pastry shell.

MAKES 4 TO 6 SERVINGS AS AN APPETIZER OR 2 SERVINGS FOR A MEAL |
COMMITMENT LEVEL: DONE IN STAGES

1 sheet commercial puff pastry or homemade Cheater's Puff Pastry (page 44), defrosted

2 onions

2 generous cups peeled and cubed butternut squash (½" cubes)

2 tablespoons olive oil

1 clove garlic

Generous pinch of salt

4 ounces chèvre or feta cheese

4–6 fresh sage leaves, minced

Fresh ground black pepper (optional)

NOTE: This kind of tart doesn't keep well, so eat up. Invite friends in or add a salad and make this a meal for 2. In the unlikely event of leftovers, wrap and refrigerate. Reheat under the broiler for a few minutes. Don't reheat in the microwave. It will be hot but soggy.

TIP: Chèvre or feta? My samplers were split down the middle. Feta is sharper and saltier, with a more pronounced flavor. Chèvre is creamier and more subtle. If chèvre is hard to find, feta is a readily available alternative. Feta is also more often made from sheep's milk; chèvre is always made from goat's milk.

1. Preheat the oven to 500°F. Line 2 rimmed baking sheets with parchment paper.

2. Remove 1 of the parchment sheets from its pan, place it on your work surface, and roll the puff pastry sheet on it to form a 10" square. Using a sharp knife, gently score the pastry an inch inside the outer edge, being careful not to cut all the way through. Return the parchment to the baking sheet, being careful not to damage the pastry during the transfer. Refrigerate while you prepare the vegetables.

3. Cut the onions in half lengthwise, place cut side down on the cutting board, and sliver vertically. Place the squash and onions in a large bowl.

4. Into a small bowl, pour the oil. Using a microplane, grate the garlic into the oil and whisk until well combined. Drizzle over the squash and onions and toss to coat thoroughly. Spoon the vegetables in a single layer onto the second baking sheet, sprinkle with salt, and roast for 15 to 20 minutes, stirring occasionally, or until the squash is browned on the outside and soft on the inside. (The filling can be prepared up to 2 days ahead of time. Just refrigerate it, covered, and then bring to room temperature before baking.)

5. Reduce the heat to 400°F. Let the vegetables cool a bit before assembling the tart. They can be warm but not piping hot when they go on the pastry.

6. Sprinkle three-quarters of the cheese onto the chilled pastry, being careful to keep inside the score marks. Spoon the roasted squash and onions on top. Sprinkle with the sage and remaining cheese. Add a grinding of black pepper, if using. Bake for 20 to 25 minutes, or until the crust is golden brown. Serve while hot.

MOROCCAN LAMB (OR BEEF) BUNDLES

These bundles capture the eclectic mix of flavors and textures that make Moroccan food so captivating. Lamb is a classic Moroccan meat, but if you can't find it, you can still enjoy the spices using ground beef.

MAKES 12 TO 16 | COMMITMENT LEVEL: DONE IN STAGES

1. *To make the filling:* In a large skillet over medium heat, heat the oil. Cook the onion until golden and soft. Add the garlic and cook for 1 minute. Add the lamb or beef, cumin, coriander, ginger, paprika, cinnamon, turmeric, pepper flakes, salt, and lemon peel. Cook until the meat is no longer pink. Transfer to a fine mesh strainer over a bowl to drain. When the meat filling has cooled, stir in the cilantro, apricots, and nuts. Because beef tends to be drier than lamb, add 1 to 2 tablespoons of the drippings back into the mixture if using beef.

2. Preheat the oven to 350°F. Get out a rimmed baking sheet. No need for parchment.

3. *To make the wrapping:* Lightly dampen a tea towel and place on top of the opened phyllo sheets to prevent the pastry from drying out. Remove 1 sheet at a time and, using a pastry brush, brush lightly with oil or butter. Fold the sheet in thirds by bringing the short sides toward the middle to make 1 long strip 3 layers thick. Place 1/4 cup of the filling at the bottom in the center, about 1/2" from the bottom edge. Fold the edge up over the filling and roll the bundle toward the top a couple of times. Fold the left and right edges over the center, and then finish rolling the bundle. Place seam side down on the baking sheet. Brush with more oil or butter. Repeat with the remaining phyllo and filling. Sprinkle the bundles with sesame seeds, if using, and bake for 20 to 25 minutes, or until the phyllo is golden and the filling is hot. Serve hot.

NOTE: Leftovers will keep for up to 4 days in the refrigerator. Reheat in a 350°F oven for 10 to 12 minutes. Resist the urge to microwave, as this will make the phyllo soggy.

TIP: Don't feel locked into making these as bundles. See pages 50–51 for different ways to use phyllo.

FILLING

1 tablespoon vegetable oil

1 onion, finely chopped

2 cloves garlic, grated on a microplane

1 pound lean ground lamb or beef

1 tablespoon ground cumin

1 teaspoon dried coriander

1/2 teaspoon ground ginger

1/2 teaspoon paprika

1/2 teaspoon ground cinnamon

1/2 teaspoon ground turmeric

1/2 teaspoon red-pepper flakes

1/2 teaspoon fine sea salt

Peel of 1/2 lemon, finely grated (about 2 teaspoons)

1/2 cup packed finely chopped cilantro

1/4 cup chopped dried apricots

1/4 cup toasted pine nuts or toasted sliced almonds

WRAPPING

1 package (16 ounces) phyllo sheets, defrosted

1/2 cup vegetable oil or melted butter

Sesame seeds, white or black (optional)

SWEET POTATO SAMOSAS

Traditional samosas are not wrapped in phyllo, but this packaged pastry is so versatile and convenient, it's the one pastry I don't bother making by hand. While this recipe calls for rolling the samosas in triangles, you can use any phyllo rolling technique that suits you. Regardless of how you wrap them, these Indian-inspired, spice-laced bundles are a perfect way to enjoy some vegetables.

MAKES ABOUT 16 | COMMITMENT LEVEL: DONE IN STAGES

1. *To make the filling:* In a large pot over high heat, boil the sweet potatoes for 3 minutes. Add the cauliflower and boil until both vegetables are tender but not falling apart. Drain and set aside.

2. In a large skillet over medium heat, heat the oil. Cook the onion for 5 minutes, or until tender and golden. Stir in the ginger and garlic and cook for 1 minute. Add the cumin, coriander, garam masala, turmeric, pepper flakes (if using), and salt. Cook for 1 minute, stirring. Gently fold in the reserved sweet potatoes and cauliflower. Stir in the coconut milk and lemon juice and cook to heat through. The filling should be moist but not wet. If there's too much moisture in the filling, the pastry will burst. If the filling is wet, continue cooking to reduce some of the liquid. If it's falling-apart dry, add a bit more coconut milk.

3. Stir in the peas and cilantro. Remove the pan from the heat and set the filling aside to let cool before folding the samosas.

4. Preheat the oven to 350°F.

5. *To make the wrapping:* Lightly dampen a tea towel and place on top of the opened phyllo sheets to prevent the pastry from drying out. Remove 1 sheet at a time and, using a pastry brush, brush lightly with oil or butter. Fold the sheet in thirds so you have a sheet about 6" × 12" and 3 layers thick. Place 1/4 cup of the filling at the bottom, about 1" from the bottom edge and slightly toward the left. Fold the bottom right corner over the filling to form a triangle. Fold the filling up, maintaining the triangle. Place the samosa on a baking sheet and brush with more oil or butter. Repeat with the remaining phyllo and filling. Dust the samosas with the sesame seeds, if using.

(continued on page 62)

FILLING

4 cups peeled and cubed sweet potatoes (about 2 large cut in 1/2" cubes)

2 cups chopped cauliflower (about 1/3 large head)

2 tablespoons vegetable oil

1 large onion, chopped

2 tablespoons grated fresh ginger

2 tablespoons grated garlic

1 tablespoon ground cumin

1 tablespoon ground coriander

1 tablespoon garam masala

1 teaspoon ground turmeric

1/2 teaspoon red-pepper flakes (optional)

1 teaspoon fine sea salt

1/2 cup unsweetened coconut milk

1/4 cup lemon juice

1 cup frozen peas (petits pois are best)

1/2 cup packed chopped cilantro

WRAPPING

1 package (16 ounces) phyllo sheets, defrosted

1/2 cup vegetable oil or melted butter

1 tablespoon black sesame seeds (optional)

(continued from page 61)

6. Bake for 20 to 25 minutes, or until the samosas are golden brown and crispy. Serve hot with mango chutney, Lime-Cilantro Dipping Sauce (page 204), or tzatziki (page 212).

NOTE: Leftovers can be refrigerated in an airtight container for up to 5 days. Reheat in a 350°F oven for 10 to 15 minutes. Microwaving will make the phyllo soggy.

TIP: The easiest way to grate ginger is to freeze the root—skin and all—in a resealable freezer bag or airtight container. When you need fresh ginger, grate the frozen ginger using a microplane. It will look like ice shavings, but within seconds, it will melt into a soft, gingery paste. There's no wood pulp to remove, no peeling required, and best of all, no waste!

CHOCOLATE-ORANGE HAZELNUT NESTS

This is my interpretation of an open-faced Ferrero Rocher chocolate. Toasted hazelnuts folded into the meringue mimic the crunchy coating, while whipped rich chocolate cream is a nod to the ganache center. A little orange brings it all together in a decadent treat worthy of any special occasion.

MAKES 8 TO 10 | COMMITMENT LEVEL: LAZY SUNDAY AFTERNOON

1. *To make the hazelnut meringue:* Preheat the oven to 200°F. Line 2 baking sheets with parchment paper.

2. In a food processor or blender, grind the hazelnuts until finely chopped. Set aside 2 tablespoons for topping.

3. In a small saucepan, combine the granulated sugar, water, and salt. Stir over high heat until the sugar dissolves. Stop stirring and bring to a boil. Boil for 2 minutes, or until ¼ teaspoon of syrup dropped into a glass of ice-cold water forms a soft ball. (This is called the soft-ball stage and is 235°F on a candy thermometer.) Remove from the heat.

4. Using a stand mixer fitted with a whisk, beat the egg whites on medium speed until foamy. Add the cream of tartar, increase the speed to medium-high, and beat until soft peaks form. With the mixer running, pour the hot sugar syrup into the eggs in a thin stream. Add the vanilla. Beat until the egg whites are stiff and glossy. Using a spatula, gently fold the chopped hazelnuts into the meringue, being careful not to overstir.

5. Drop the meringue onto the baking sheets in mounds. Create an indentation in the middle using the back of a spoon or an ice cream scoop dipped in water. The aim is to create a nest that will hold the cream.

6. Bake for 2 hours. Turn off the heat and leave in the oven for 1 hour with the door slightly ajar.

7. *To make the Chocolate-Orange Cream:* In a medium bowl, sift the confectioners' sugar and cocoa together. In a large bowl, pour the cream. Whisk the confectioners' sugar mixture into the cream. Add the orange liqueur and peel. Using an electric mixer on high speed, beat until soft peaks form. Cover and refrigerate until needed.

8. When the meringues are cool, fill each nest with a generous scoop of chocolate-orange cream. Dust with the reserved hazelnuts. Serve immediately.

HAZELNUT MERINGUE

1¼ cups toasted hazelnuts, skins removed

1 cup granulated sugar

¼ cup water

Pinch of fine sea salt

4 egg whites

¼ teaspoon cream of tartar

1 teaspoon pure vanilla extract

CHOCOLATE-ORANGE CREAM

1 cup sifted confectioners' sugar

½ cup sifted unsweetened cocoa powder

2 cups heavy cream

2 tablespoons orange liqueur

Peel of 1 large orange, finely grated (about 2 tablespoons)

NOTE: The meringues won't keep once the cream is added, so assemble only as many as you are going to eat. Store leftover unfilled meringues in an airtight container. Leftover cream, if covered and refrigerated immediately, will keep for 2 to 3 days.

TIP: You can use the leftover egg yolks to make crème anglaise (page 222) or aioli (page 207).

VANILLA-SCENTED PALMIERS

With the exception of lemon pie, these are my father's all-time favorite dessert; he likes them without chocolate. I like them with. Or without. Either way, these are not the bready imposters found in many North American bakeries. Simple, flaky, sweet, and buttery, these are the shattery treats sold at tiny French patisseries that line cobblestone streets. One bite and you'll think you're in Paris.

MAKES 24 | COMMITMENT LEVEL: DONE IN STAGES

¾ cup vanilla sugar (see recipe for "The Slow Way" on page 39) or plain granulated sugar

1 rectangle homemade Cheater's Puff Pastry (page 44) or 1 roll commercial puff pastry

4 ounces semisweet chocolate, chopped (optional)

1. Sprinkle the work surface with half the sugar. Place the puff pastry on the sugar. Sprinkle with more sugar. Pressing the sugar into the dough, roll until you have an 8" × 12" rectangle. If using homemade pastry, flip and turn the dough often to ensure lots of sugar gets worked into the surface of the dough.

2. Trim the dough so that the edges are even and set the trimmings aside for later. Fold the long sides of the pastry rectangle toward the center. Don't have these edges touch. Instead, leave ½" between where the folded edges would meet. This gap is crucial for the palmiers to keep their shape when cooking.

3. Fold the dough in half along this gap. You will now have a roll 4 layers thick and about 2" wide and 12" long. Flatten the dough gently with the palms of your hands, wrap in plastic wrap, and refrigerate for 1 to 2 hours. Scrape the sugar off the work surface and save with the rest of the sugar for dipping later.

4. About 30 minutes before you are ready to bake the palmiers, preheat the oven to 375°F. Line a baking sheet or two with parchment paper.

5. With a sharp knife, cut the dough crosswise ½" thick. Dip both cut sides in the sugar and place cut side down on the baking sheets. Be sure to leave at least 2" between palmiers. They will expand quite a bit sideways. They don't expand much up and down, so you might be able to get 6 rows of 4 if your sheet is big enough.

6. Bake for 15 to 20 minutes, or until the palmiers are golden around the edges and the sugar has caramelized. Allow to cool for a few minutes before transferring to a rack to cool fully.

(continued on page 67)

(continued from page 64)

7. While the palmiers are baking, roll the reserved ends in sugar and cut into bite-size pieces. When the "real" palmiers are cooling, bake the ends for 10 to 15 minutes, or until golden and caramelized. They will look odd but will taste just as good. Don't serve these. Reserve them for yourself as a treat for your hard work.

8. *Optional chocolate dip:* Melt the chocolate in the microwave oven in 30-second bursts or in a heatproof bowl over hot, not boiling, water, stirring gently until smooth. (For more on melting chocolate, see page 28.) Tilting the bowl to pool the melted chocolate, dip half of a palmier into the liquid chocolate, then place on parchment paper or waxed paper to set. Repeat with the remaining palmiers and chocolate.

NOTE: Palmiers are best eaten the day they are made. Store leftovers in an airtight container. Do not freeze baked palmiers. Their sugar content is too high.

TIP: Ever wonder why some cookies freeze well and others don't? Sugar softens once frozen, so cookies with a high sugar content or crispy caramelized surfaces will just get soggy.

CHERRY AND LEMON MACAROON MERINGUES

Meringues and macaroons are usually gluten free. Paired together, they make an irresistible dessert even my wheat-eating friends can't pass up. This recipe is inspired by a date-filled macaroon from Blackbird Bakery Gluten-Free *by Karen Morgan. In this version, tart dried cherries and slightly bitter walnuts bring the sugar and coconut into balance, while lemon peel rounds out the flavor. As with Morgan's version, you'll need a napkin. They leave a trail of meringue flakes wherever you eat them.*

MAKES ABOUT 3 DOZEN | COMMITMENT LEVEL: LAZY SUNDAY AFTERNOON

1 cup sugar

1½ teaspoons cornstarch

4 egg whites, at room temperature

1½ teaspoons pure vanilla extract

Peel of 1 lemon, finely grated

¾ teaspoon white vinegar

2 tablespoons boiling water

1 cup chopped dried unsweetened
   cherries

1 cup finely chopped walnuts

3 cups sweetened shredded coconut

NOTE: Store in an airtight container in a cool, dry place for up to 1 week—if they last that long.

Variations: This cookie has endless options.

- Swap dried cranberries or Craisins for the dried cherries and orange peel instead of lemon.
- Try lime peel instead of lemon and dried pineapple instead of cherries for a piña colada meringue.

1. Line 2 baking sheets with parchment paper or silicone baking mats. Preheat the oven to 350°F with the baking rack in the center.

2. In a small bowl, combine the sugar and cornstarch.

3. In the bowl of a stand mixer fitted with a whisk, beat the egg whites on high speed until foamy. (You can use a hand mixer, but it will take longer.) Reduce the speed to medium and add the sugar mixture 1 tablespoon at a time. Once the sugar has been fully incorporated, increase the speed to high. Add the vanilla, lemon peel, and vinegar and continue beating until the egg whites form stiff, glossy peaks.

4. Reduce the speed to medium and add the boiling water. Don't panic. The egg whites are supposed to swell up. Once the egg whites settle down again, beat for 2 minutes on high. Set the meringue aside.

5. In a large bowl, combine the dried cherries, walnuts, and coconut. Toss to ensure the ingredients are evenly distributed. You want to avoid overstirring the meringue, so do your mixing now.

6. Sprinkle the fruit-and-nut mixture over the surface of the meringue. Using a scraper, gently fold it into the meringue. Using a 1-tablespoon cookie scoop, drop mounds of macaroons 1" apart on the baking sheets. Alternatively, you can do this with a spoon and slide the batter off with your finger. They will have more of a peak but will taste just as good.

7. Bake 1 sheet at a time on the middle rack for 5 minutes. Reduce the heat to 225°F and bake for 40 to 45 minutes, or until the cookies are light gold. Remove from the oven and allow to cool for 15 minutes. When they are stable enough to be removed without damage, transfer the cookies to a rack to cool completely. Repeat with the remaining cookies.

CRUMBLY

delicious treats that crumble when you eat them

My mother always knew when I had been sneaking goodies. Although the evidence had been washed away with greedy gulps of milk, there was no fooling her. She'd point to the crumbs—on the counter, on my clothes, on the corners of my mouth, on the palms of my hand. Busted. Stupid crumbs. Tattletales.

Today I view them as a barometer of a dish's success. In a glance, I can tell which muffins were taken into a quiet corner to be eaten undisturbed and which were devoured right at the serving plate. I'm most proud of crumbs by the front door, eaten by friends taking "one for the road," biting the last brownie before giving a hug and crumb-studded kiss good-bye.

CRUMBLY

SAVORY

SWEET

BASIL AND AGED CHEDDAR SCONES

At the Wild Flour Bakery in Banff, Alberta, an artisanal café with a spectacular view of the Rocky Mountains, I had a scone so good, I stopped my mountain gazing, pulled out my notepad, and jotted down flavor notes. Like the view-stopping Rocky Mountain scones, these are full of fresh basil, have a kiss of sugar, and provide a burst of sharp Cheddar. The only thing missing? Fresh mountain air and a bowl of tomato soup.

MAKES 12 | COMMITMENT LEVEL: READY IN AN HOUR OR LESS

2¼ cups all-purpose flour

¼ cup sugar

1 tablespoon baking powder

½ teaspoon baking soda

½ teaspoon fine sea salt

½ cup cold butter, cubed

1 cup roughly chopped fresh basil

4 ounces grated aged Cheddar cheese (about 1 cup)

1 cup buttermilk

TIP: If you don't have buttermilk on hand, sour your own. Place 1 tablespoon of lemon juice or white vinegar in a measuring cup. Fill to the 1-cup mark with milk and let sit for 10 minutes. Stir and use immediately.

1. Preheat the oven to 425°F.

2. *Hand method:* In a large bowl, combine the flour, sugar, baking powder, baking soda, and salt. Using a pastry blender or 2 knives, cut the butter in until it's the size of peas. Chop the basil finely and stir into the flour mixture to evenly distribute.

   Food processor method: In the bowl of a food processor fitted with a steel blade, combine the flour, sugar, baking powder, baking soda, and salt with a few pulses. Add the basil. Pulse in 2-second bursts until the basil is chopped and evenly distributed. Add the butter and pulse until it's about the size of peas. Transfer the flour mixture to a large bowl.

3. Add the cheese and toss to evenly distribute. Add the buttermilk and stir until the dough forms a ball. Knead the dough on a floured surface until it just comes together. Roll into a round about 10″ wide and ¾″ thick. Cut into 12 wedges. Place on an ungreased baking sheet about 2″ apart and bake for 12 to 15 minutes, or until golden. Serve immediately.

NOTE: Scones can be stored in an airtight container for up to 3 days but are really best within a few hours of baking. To reheat, split in half and pop under the broiler. Serve with butter.

ROSEMARY AND CARAMELIZED ONION FOCACCIA

I can buy freshly baked focaccia just down the street. It's delicious, and the smell is so tempting, it's hard to resist—until I see the $8-per-loaf price tag. I figured this meant the bread is hard to make. It isn't. All you need is a bit of patience with the onions. Not only does homemade focaccia cost a fraction of the bakery version, it's easy to customize. My half has rosemary and onions. My husband has no rosemary and extra onions. Everybody wins.

MAKES 1, SERVES 8 | COMMITMENT LEVEL: DONE IN STAGES

FOCACCIA DOUGH

1 package (2¼ teaspoons) instant dry yeast

3 cups all-purpose flour, divided

¾ teaspoon fine sea salt

¾ cup water

½ cup milk

2 tablespoons olive oil

TOPPINGS

2 tablespoons olive oil, plus more for drizzling

3 large onions, thinly sliced

2 tablespoons minced fresh rosemary

Coarse kosher salt

Fresh cracked black pepper

1. *To make the focaccia dough:* In a stand mixer fitted with a paddle or in a large bowl using a wooden spoon, combine the yeast, 1 cup of the flour, and the salt. In a small pan over medium-low heat, combine the water and milk and gently heat until they are just warmer than your finger (about 110°F). Add the oil to the milk mixture and whisk to combine. Add to the flour mixture and beat on medium speed for 2 minutes. Add the remaining 2 cups flour, ½ cup at a time, until the dough pulls away from the side of the bowl. When it becomes too hard to mix by hand, turn onto a floured surface and knead in the flour. For either method, knead the dough until it is smooth and elastic.

2. Oil a large bowl, place the dough in the bowl, and turn the dough to coat it with the oil. Cover with plastic wrap and leave to double at room temperature, about 90 minutes. Line a 10″ × 15″ rimmed baking sheet with parchment paper.

3. *To make the toppings:* While the dough is rising, caramelize the onions. In a large skillet over medium heat, heat the oil. Cook the onions slowly, stirring occasionally. This takes time—a good 30 to 40 minutes. Do not try to rush the process. You might have to lower the heat to ensure the onions don't brown too quickly. Continue cooking and stirring the onions until they are a golden brown. You want to slightly under-caramelize them, as they will continue to crisp when the focaccia bakes.

4. Turn the dough onto a floured surface and knead a few times. Place on the baking sheet and stretch to fit the pan. Cover with a tea towel and let rise for 30 to 45 minutes. While the dough is rising, preheat the oven to 400°F.

5. When the dough has risen, use your fingers to poke dimples in it, no more than $\frac{1}{4}$" deep. Drizzle the surface with oil. Sprinkle with the onions, rosemary, some kosher salt, and a good grinding of black pepper. Press the toppings gently into the dough with the palm of your hand to secure them.

6. Bake for 20 to 25 minutes, or until golden brown. Allow to cool on the baking sheet for 5 minutes before transferring to a rack. The focaccia may be eaten slightly warm.

NOTE: Focaccia is best eaten the day it's baked. If you have leftover focaccia, split it in half lengthwise, brush it with a bit of olive oil, and pop under the broiler for new life.

TIP: If you adore caramelized onions, make a big batch and store leftovers in the refrigerator for up to 5 days or freeze them for up to 3 months. Sprinkle them on Crispy-Crust Pizza (page 156), or add a few atop a serving of Bacon, Cheddar, and Thyme Waffles (page 148).

STUFFED TOMATO, ARUGULA, AND CILANTRO FOCACCIA

Whether the sun, the oven, or a dehydrator does the work, dried tomatoes deliver a concentrated hit of flavor to dishes without adding moisture. For this stuffed focaccia, use any form of dried tomatoes you can find, but resist the urge to simply chop up cherry or grape tomatoes. They will make the bread soggy and won't provide the sweetness needed to balance the bite of the arugula.

MAKES 1 FOCACCIA, SERVES 8 | COMMITMENT LEVEL: DONE IN STAGES

FOCACCIA DOUGH

1 package (2¼ teaspoons) instant dry yeast

3 cups all-purpose flour, divided

¾ teaspoon fine sea salt

¾ cup water

½ cup milk

2 tablespoons olive oil

TOPPINGS

Cornmeal, for sprinkling

2 cups baby arugula (or baby spinach)

½ cup chopped fresh cilantro

½ cup dried tomatoes, slivered

½ cup grated Parmesan cheese

Olive oil, for topping

Coarse sea or kosher salt

Fresh cracked black pepper

NOTE: Focaccia is best eaten the day it's baked. If you have leftover focaccia, pop it under the broiler for new life.

TIP: If you find sun-dried tomatoes hard to cut, snip them with kitchen scissors.

1. *To make the focaccia dough:* In a stand mixer fitted with a paddle or in a large bowl using a wooden spoon, combine the yeast, 1 cup of the flour, and the salt. In a small saucepan over medium-low heat, combine the water and milk and gently heat until just warm (about 110°F). Add the oil and whisk to combine. Pour evenly over the flour mixture and beat on medium speed for 2 minutes. Add the remaining 2 cups flour, ½ cup at a time, until the dough pulls away from the side of the bowl. If mixing by hand, when it becomes too hard to mix, turn onto a floured surface and knead in the flour. Knead until the dough is smooth and elastic.

2. Oil a large bowl, place the dough in the bowl, and turn the dough to coat it with the oil. Cover with plastic wrap and leave to double at room temperature, about 90 minutes.

3. *To prepare the toppings:* While the dough rises, line a 10" × 15" rimmed baking sheet with parchment paper and sprinkle lightly with cornmeal. If using oil-packed sun-dried tomatoes, drain them.

4. Turn the dough onto a large, lightly floured cutting board and divide the dough in half. Roll 1 piece into a 10" × 15" rectangle. Slide the dough off the board onto the baking sheet; press the dough so it covers the bottom and sides. Sprinkle half each of the arugula, cilantro, tomatoes, and cheese over the surface. Drizzle with a bit of oil. Roll the second piece of dough into a 10" x 15" rectangle and slide it on top of the first, pinching the sides to seal. Sprinkle with oil and top with the remaining arugula, cilantro, tomatoes, and cheese. Add a sprinkle of coarse salt and fresh cracked pepper. Let rise, uncovered, for 40 minutes. While the dough is rising, preheat the oven to 400°F.

5. Bake for 20 to 25 minutes, or until golden brown. Allow to cool on the baking sheet for 5 minutes before transferring to a rack to continue cooling. Eat while still warm.

PIGLET MUFFINS WITH CARAMELIZED BACON

When I was a kid, I was crazy for all things Winnie the Pooh. When lunchtime got fussy, my ever-so-wise mom served up Piglets. These were just open-faced grilled cheese sandwiches with a slice of cut-up bacon on top. Telling me "This is what Piglet eats for lunch" put an end to all the fussing. Wanting to do something Pigletty for this book, I kept the basic flavors but gave them an adult twist via a savory muffin studded with smoked Cheddar and crunchy bits of caramelized bacon. Piglets—just like Mom used to make, only smokier, crunchier, and waaaay more crumbly.

MAKES 12 | COMMITMENT LEVEL: READY IN AN HOUR OR LESS (IF YOU HAVE CARAMELIZED BACON ON HAND) | DONE IN STAGES (IF YOU DON'T)

1. Preheat the oven to 350°F. Line a 12-cup muffin pan with paper liners.

2. In a large bowl, combine the flour, sugar, baking powder, baking soda, salt, and pepper. Add the cheese and bacon and toss to coat evenly.

3. In a medium bowl, whisk together the buttermilk, eggs, and butter. Pour over the flour mixture and stir until just blended. The batter will be thick, almost sconelike.

4. Spoon evenly into the lined muffin cups. Bake for 18 to 20 minutes, or until a wooden pick inserted in the center comes out clean. Cool in the muffin pan on a rack for 5 minutes. When cool enough to handle, remove the muffins from the pan. Eat while still warm, with or without butter.

NOTE: Store in an airtight container in the refrigerator for up to 5 days. To rewarm, split and pop under the broiler until golden. Microwaving will make them soggy.

2 cups all-purpose flour

1 tablespoon sugar

1 tablespoon baking powder

$\frac{1}{2}$ teaspoon baking soda

$\frac{1}{2}$ teaspoon fine sea salt

$\frac{1}{8}$ teaspoon fresh cracked black pepper

6 ounces grated smoked Cheddar cheese (about $1\frac{1}{2}$ cups)

6 slices caramelized bacon, broken into $\frac{1}{4}$" pieces (page 82, but extra-crispy regular bacon will do in a pinch)

1 cup buttermilk

2 eggs, at room temperature

$\frac{1}{4}$ cup melted unsalted butter

TIP: Fill the muffin cups using a $\frac{1}{4}$-cup cookie scoop. Being the same size, they will cook evenly. Plus, they'll have a lovely rounded top.

CARAMELIZED BACON

Make a bunch of this ahead of time and keep on hand for when the urge to make Piglet Muffins (page 81) strikes.

MAKES 4–6 SERVINGS | COMMITMENT LEVEL: READY IN AN HOUR OR LESS

1 pound sliced bacon (thick cut is best but regular will do)

1 cup packed dark brown sugar

Generous amount of fresh ground black pepper (optional)

1. Place oven racks in the upper and lower thirds of the oven. Preheat the oven to 400°F, using the convection setting if you have that option. Line 2 heavy, rimmed baking pans with foil or parchment paper.

2. Separate the bacon strips and place in a single layer on the pans. They can touch but shouldn't overlap. Sprinkle each pan with half the sugar. Give each pan a generous grinding of black pepper, if using. Gently pat the sugar onto the bacon so it's evenly coated.

3. Bake for 20 to 25 minutes, or until the bacon is crisp. The sugar will melt and spread, so you don't have to turn the bacon over during baking. However, if you don't have a convection oven, you will want to rotate the pans half-way through cooking to ensure even baking. The bacon is done when the sugar is melted and bubbly and the bacon looks dark brown but not burned.

4. Remove the pans from the oven. Transfer individual slices to a rack set over paper towels to absorb any drips. When the bacon cools, the sugar will harden to a thin, hard-candy coating. Eat, use in a recipe immediately, or store in the refrigerator in a resealable plastic bag between layers of parchment paper for no longer than 3 days.

SAVORY PECAN AND CHEDDAR BITES

This recipe changed the way I bake—or at least the way I label baking. You'd think nearly 3 dozen biscuits tucked in the freezer behind containers of homemade soup stock and sliced peaches would be safe for a few days. Nope. My husband quietly finished off an entire batch on his own, sneaking a handful here and there. These rich, savory biscuits are like one of those decadent, irresistible, nut-coated cheese balls, only in a crisp cookie-shaped form. Think of them as a cracker and cheese replacement and enjoy them with a glass of sherry or scotch in front of the fire. Now, if I have future plans for any food item, above the dish's name and date, I add the not-so-subtle note "Hands off!" Sometimes even that doesn't work.

MAKES ABOUT 2½ DOZEN | COMMITMENT LEVEL: DONE IN STAGES

1. In a small bowl, whisk together the flour, red pepper, and mustard to thoroughly combine.

2. In a large bowl, cream the butter with a wooden spoon until soft. Gradually blend in the cheese and pecans. Alternatively, you can do this in a stand mixer fitted with a paddle.

3. Add the flour mixture ¼ cup at a time, working it in well after each addition. You might have to blend the mixture with your hands to form a doughy ball.

4. Place the dough on a sheet of waxed paper or plastic wrap. Shape the dough with your hands to form a log about 2″ in diameter. Wrap in the paper or plastic and gently roll with your palms to smooth the outside of the dough. Chill for 1 hour, or until firm. This can be done the day before if you like.

5. Preheat the oven to 400°F. Cut the dough into rounds ¼″ thick. Arrange slightly apart on a baking sheet. Bake for 8 to 10 minutes, or until they begin to turn golden around the edges. Remove from the baking sheet at once and cool on a rack.

NOTE: Store in an airtight container for up to 3 days at room temperature or a week in the refrigerator. Allow to come to room temperature before eating.

1 cup all-purpose flour

Generous pinch of ground red pepper

½ teaspoon dry mustard

½ cup salted butter, at room temperature

6 ounces shredded aged Cheddar cheese (about 1½ cups)

½ cup chopped pecans

TIP: The unbaked dough can be frozen for up to a month before being defrosted and baked. The finished biscuits can be frozen for up to 2 months.

BLUEBERRY–LIME CORNMEAL MUFFINS

Talk about messy: These are not pack-in-your-lunch-bag muffins. They're more have-a-cup-of-tea-and-a-nice-chat muffins. Although the cornmeal base is studded with blueberries, lime is the anchor. It balances the sweetness of the cornmeal, brightens the freshness of the blueberries, and smooths the edges of the honey. With its own glaze and butter, lime works its way into every layer of this deliciously messy muffin.

MAKES 18 | COMMITMENT LEVEL: READY IN AN HOUR OR LESS

1. *To make the muffins:* Preheat the oven to 400°F. Line 18 muffin cups with paper or parchment liners.

2. In a large bowl, sift together the flour, cornmeal, baking powder, baking soda, and salt.

3. In a medium bowl, mix together the granulated sugar, brown sugar, egg, buttermilk, butter, vanilla, and lime peel.

4. Add the blueberries to the flour mixture and toss to coat. Pour the buttermilk mixture over the flour mixture and, using a spatula, mix until the batter is just combined. Don't overmix.

5. Using a ¼-cup scoop, fill the muffin cups. Bake for 17 to 20 minutes, or until the muffins are golden brown and a wooden pick inserted in the center comes out clean. While the muffins are baking, make the glaze and whipped butter (if using).

6. *To make the glaze:* In a small bowl, mix the sugar, lime juice, and lime peel until the sugar is dissolved. Set aside. Stir well just before using.

7. *To make the whipped butter:* In a small bowl, using an electric mixer on low speed, blend the butter, honey, lime peel, and lime juice. With the electric mixer on high speed, whip for 3 minutes, or until light and fluffy. Add salt to taste.

8. Allow the muffins to cool for a few minutes in the pans before transferring to a rack. While still warm, dip the tops of the muffins into the glaze. Turn upright, poke a few holes in the tops with a skewer, and spoon the remaining glaze evenly over the muffins. Allow to cool. Serve with regular butter or whipped honey-lime butter.

NOTE: These muffins will keep in an airtight container in the refrigerator for a couple of days. If they last that long.

2 cups all-purpose flour

1 cup fine ground cornmeal

2 teaspoons baking powder

1 teaspoon baking soda

½ teaspoon fine sea salt

¾ cup granulated sugar

¼ cup brown sugar

1 egg, at room temperature

1 cup buttermilk

¾ cup melted butter

1 teaspoon pure vanilla extract

Peel of 1 lime, finely grated

1½ cups fresh or frozen unthawed blueberries (wild, if you can get them)

LIME GLAZE

½ cup granulated sugar

¼ cup fresh lime juice

Peel of 1 lime, finely grated

WHIPPED HONEY–LIME BUTTER (OPTIONAL)

½ cup butter, at room temperature

1 tablespoon honey

Peel of 1 lime, finely grated

1 tablespoon fresh lime juice

Generous pinch of fine sea salt

LEMONY STRAWBERRY-PEACH MUFFINS

Whoever developed the ever-bearing strawberry should be given Lemony Strawberry-Peach Muffins for life and be named Matchmaker of the Year. Thanks to the breakthrough that extended berry season, local strawberries can finally meet their soul mate—peaches. In a classic case of "opposites attract," diminutive seed-speckled berries unite with voluptuous stone fruit. A bit of lemon acts as chaperone to keep things from getting out of hand. The result is a sweet, tender muffin dotted with color and capped with a crunchy sugar top. Based on extended observation, I think these crazy kids just might make it.

MAKES 12 | COMMITMENT LEVEL: READY IN AN HOUR OR LESS

1 small peach

$1/2$ cup sliced strawberries

$1/2$ cup granulated sugar

$1/2$ cup butter, at room temperature

Peel of 1 lemon, finely grated

2 eggs, at room temperature

1 teaspoon pure vanilla extract

$1 1/2$ cups all-purpose flour

1 teaspoon baking powder

$1/2$ teaspoon baking soda

$1/4$ teaspoon fine sea salt

$1/2$ cup buttermilk

2 tablespoons turbinado sugar

TIP: If possible, slice the fruit chilled. It will reduce the amount of juice you lose.

1. Preheat the oven to 375°F. Line a 12-cup muffin pan with paper liners.

2. Peel and chop the peach into a strainer placed over a bowl to catch the juices (you should have $1/2$ cup chopped peach). Too much juice will make the batter soggy. Don't discard the juice. Put it in a smoothie or drink it as is. Add the strawberries to the peaches and toss to evenly distribute.

3. In a large bowl, either by hand or using an electric mixer on high speed, beat the granulated sugar, butter, and lemon peel until light and fluffy. Add the eggs and vanilla and beat until well combined.

4. In a medium bowl, combine the flour, baking powder, baking soda, and salt. With a spoon or spatula, stir the flour mixture into the butter mixture, alternating with the buttermilk, beginning and ending with the flour. With each addition, stir only until the ingredients are combined. Gently fold in the fruit. Do not overmix.

5. Using a $1/4$-cup scoop, fill the muffin cups. Top with a generous sprinkle of turbinado sugar. Bake for 25 minutes, or until a wooden pick inserted in the center comes out clean. Cool in the pan for 5 minutes before transferring to a rack to cool completely.

NOTE: Store muffins in an airtight container in the refrigerator for up to 3 days.

GINGER AND VANILLA SCONES

Many scones are merely a delivery system for jam and clotted cream. But these? They need little more than a kiss of butter and a thank-you. Sweet and tender, these scones maintain their clear vanilla base even though they're packed with chewy bits of candied ginger. If you must top them with something beyond butter, try a dab of gentle pear-and-ginger conserve or a smear of local flower honey.

MAKES 12 | COMMITMENT LEVEL: READY IN AN HOUR OR LESS

1. Preheat the oven to 425°F.

2. *Hand method:* In a large bowl, mix the flour, sugar, baking powder, baking soda, and salt. Using a pastry blender or 2 knives, cut the butter in until it's the size of peas.

   Food processor method: In the bowl of a food processor fitted with a steel blade, combine the flour, sugar, baking powder, baking soda, and salt with a few pulses. Add the butter and pulse until it's the size of peas. Transfer the flour mixture to a large bowl.

3. By hand, stir the ginger into the flour mixture, tossing well to distribute evenly.

4. Stir the vanilla into the buttermilk. Pour over the flour mixture and stir until the dough forms a ball. On a floured surface, knead the dough until it just comes together. Roll until it's ³⁄₄" thick. Using a biscuit cutter or glass, cut into 3" circles. Gather the leftover dough, roll it again quickly, and cut more circles. Don't roll a third time or the scones will be tough. Don't throw out the leftover dough, though. Instead, use your fingers to squish the scattered bits into one final lumpy scone. Our family calls this the ugly scone, but for all its lumps, we fight for who gets the privilege to eat it.

5. Place the scones on an ungreased baking sheet and bake for 12 to 15 minutes, or until golden. Serve immediately.

NOTE: Scones are best eaten right away. Leftovers can be stored in an airtight container for up to 5 days. To reheat, split the scone open and pop it under the broiler. Serve with butter and jam.

2¼ cups all-purpose flour

¼ cup sugar (vanilla sugar if you have it, page 39)

1 tablespoon baking powder

½ teaspoon baking soda

½ teaspoon fine sea salt

½ cup cold butter, cubed

1 cup minced crystallized ginger

1 tablespoon pure vanilla extract

1 cup buttermilk

TIP: For a quick breakfast, mix together the dry ingredients and cut in the butter the night before. Store the butter-and-flour mixture in the fridge overnight. In the morning, add the wet ingredients and cut the scones while the oven heats.

WELSH GRIDDLE CAKES

*This recipe emerged from hibernation when I temporarily moved in with my parents during a kitchen reno-
vation that took over our small house. Taking advantage of our time together, Mom pulled out old, nearly
forgotten family recipes. While we chatted, she diligently rolled out the dough, cut it into squares, and
cooked the griddle cakes. We ate them with tea. When the tea was gone, we ate them with a smear of butter
and a scrape of ginger marmalade. The sweet currants, bits of ginger, and gentle spices combine in an old-
fashioned treat that is nearly impossible to resist. Comforting and approachable, this is one of my most
requested recipes. Although we never have enough when people drop by for tea, you can halve this recipe.*

MAKES 4 TO 5 DOZEN | COMMITMENT LEVEL: READY IN AN HOUR OR LESS

3 cups all-purpose flour

1 cup sugar

1½ teaspoons baking powder

1 teaspoon fine sea salt

½ teaspoon baking soda

1 teaspoon freshly ground nutmeg

¼ teaspoon ground mace

1 cup cold unsalted butter, cubed

1 cup currants

¾ cup finely chopped crystallized ginger

2 eggs, at room temperature

6 tablespoons milk

TIP: Mace is the outer skin
of nutmeg. It's a bit spunkier
than nutmeg, with hints of
clove and pepper. If you can't
find it, substitute the same
amount of nutmeg, allspice, or
apple pie spice.

1. In a large bowl, whisk together the flour, sugar, baking powder, salt, baking soda, nutmeg, and mace.

2. Using a pastry blender or 2 knives, cut in the butter until it resembles coarse crumbs. Add the currants and ginger and toss lightly to coat thoroughly with the flour mixture.

3. In a small bowl, whisk the eggs and milk together until well combined. Pour over the dry ingredients. Mix to make a stiff dough. Divide the dough in half.

4. Heat an ungreased griddle or a large nonstick frying pan (or 2) over medium-low heat. Alternatively, you can set an electric frying pan to 250°F. You might have to fiddle with the heat to find the "sweet spot" for your griddle or pans. This is a make-again recipe.

5. On a floured surface, roll the first half of dough to a square approximately 10″ × 10″ and ¼″ thick. Cut into 2″-wide squares.

6. Cook the cakes for 8 to 10 minutes, turning once, or until golden brown and cooked all the way through. While the griddle cakes are cooking, roll and cut the second half of the dough. Serve hot or cold.

NOTE: Griddle cakes will keep in an airtight container for up to a week.

Variation: Swap chopped dried cranberries for the currants.

DEEP DARK CHERRY AND CHIPOTLE BROWNIES

I first learned about the chocolate-chile combination when I saw the movie Chocolat. *I was so intrigued that I raced home to make a cup of chile-laced hot chocolate just to test the theory. No matter that I'd attended the late show. Curiosity won out over sleep. I've been playing with variations of this duo ever since. A rich, chewy brownie seemed the perfect platform. The tartness of the cherries plays against the smoky warmth of the chile, and it's all wrapped up in a rich, deep dark chocolate brownie.*

MAKES 20 | COMMITMENT LEVEL: READY IN AN HOUR OR LESS

1. Preheat the oven to 350°F. Line a 9″ × 9″ baking pan with an extra-long piece of foil that hangs over opposite edges. Coat with cooking spray.

2. In a medium bowl, melt the chocolate, milk, and butter together gently. You can do this in the microwave on medium power in 60-second bursts, stirring in between. Alternatively, you can place the chocolate, milk, and butter in a heatproof bowl over a pot of simmering water and stir gently until all the ingredients are dissolved.

3. Into a large bowl, sift the flour, cocoa, and baking powder. Add the chile pepper, salt, granulated sugar, and brown sugar and stir until well blended. Add the cherries and toss to coat with the flour mixture. This way they won't sink to the bottom while baking.

4. Whisk the vanilla into the eggs. Add to the melted chocolate mixture and stir to combine. Pour into the flour mixture and stir to combine. Pour the batter into the pan, pushing the batter to the edges.

5. Bake for 35 minutes, or until a wooden pick inserted halfway between the side and the center comes out clean. Allow the brownies to cool on a rack before removing from the pan using the foil overhang. Do not turn the brownies out upside down. They will not survive being uprighted. Instead, leave the brownies in the foil and cut them into squares as needed. Leaving the pan of brownies intact as long as you can helps keep them moist. Serve with vanilla bean ice cream or a dollop of crème fraîche (page 224) or with nothing else at all.

NOTE: To store, just wrap the foil around the brownies and store in an airtight container or a resealable plastic bag with the air squeezed out.

2 ounces bittersweet chocolate, coarsely chopped

1/3 cup milk

6 tablespoons unsalted butter

3/4 cup all-purpose flour

3/4 cup unsweetened cocoa powder

1/2 teaspoon baking powder

1 teaspoon ground chipotle chile pepper (1/2 teaspoon if you want only a hint of heat)

1/4 teaspoon fine sea salt

1 cup granulated sugar

1/2 cup packed brown sugar

1 cup chopped dried tart cherries

1 teaspoon pure vanilla extract

2 eggs, at room temperature

TIP: You can vary the flavors.

- Try cinnamon or ground ancho chile pepper instead of the chipotle.
- Substitute walnuts for half of the dried cherries.

DIPPABLE

treats you dunk in coffee, tea, milk, soups, or sauces

When solid meets liquid, delicious changes occur. Rock-hard biscotti relax with a sigh when slipped into hot coffee or a steaming bowl of soup. Thirsty cookies lap up milk or cider or hot chocolate. Even vegetable chips grab on to sauces for dear life.

Will dipping lead to spills? Quite likely. But these dishes were designed to be dunked. Bathe your biscotti, douse your roasted cauliflower, immerse a cheese twist, and saturate a cigarette. Go on. Take the plunge.

DIPPABLE

SAVORY

SWEET

HERB, OLIVE, AND PARMESAN BISCOTTI

Forget the cappuccino. These savory biscotti are made for soup, stews, or piping hot bowls of chili. Think of them as chunky croutons or hearty, olive-and-nut-studded breadsticks. They're flavorful enough to stand on their own, but I love how they soften when slipped beneath the surface of a creamy tomato soup.

MAKES ABOUT 40 | COMMITMENT LEVEL: DONE IN STAGES

$3/4$ cup chopped walnuts

$1/2$ cup unsalted butter, at room temperature

2 tablespoons sugar

Peel of 1 lemon, finely grated

2 eggs, slightly beaten, at room temperature

1 large clove garlic, grated on a microplane

$1/4$ cup 2% milk

$3/4$ cup roughly chopped black olives

2 cups all-purpose flour

2 tablespoons finely minced fresh rosemary

1 teaspoon fresh coarsely ground black pepper

$1 1/2$ teaspoons baking powder

$1/2$ teaspoon fine sea salt

1 cup grated Parmesan cheese

TIP: This recipe can be halved. You can also swap pine nuts or pecans for the walnuts.

1. Preheat the oven to 350°F. Line a large baking sheet with parchment paper.

2. Once the oven comes up to heat, toast the walnuts on an unlined baking sheet for 10 minutes, or until fragrant. Set aside to cool.

3. Meanwhile, using an electric or stand mixer with a paddle attachment, cream the butter, sugar, and lemon peel until light in color. Add the eggs, garlic, and milk and beat until blended. Stir in the olives.

4. In a medium bowl, whisk together the flour, rosemary, pepper, baking powder, salt, reserved walnuts, and cheese. With the mixer on low or using a wooden spoon, mix the flour mixture into the butter mixture, stirring until just blended.

5. Divide the dough in half. Using floured hands, shape each half into a log about 12″ long. The logs will be oilier than normal biscotti if you used olives stored in oil. Place on the parchment-lined baking sheet and flatten to 1″ high. Bake for 25 to 35 minutes, or until the tops feel firm when lightly pressed. Remove the pan from the oven, reduce the heat to 325°F, and let the logs cool for at least 15 minutes on the baking sheet.

6. Transfer the logs to a cutting board. Using a serrated knife, cut 1 log on the diagonal into slices about $1/2$″ thick. Place cut side down on a baking sheet and bake for 10 minutes. Turn the biscotti over and bake for 5 to 10 minutes, or until they start to brown. Transfer to a rack to cool and maintain their crispness. Repeat with the second log. You can reuse the parchment if you like.

NOTE: Store in an airtight container for up to a week. Biscotti freeze well for up to 2 months.

CHILI CHEESE TWISTS

My mother used to serve a cheese-only version of these at parties. I thought they were the epitome of sophistication, as they made the rounds on a doily-lined tray alongside the smoked oyster spread. This spiced variation has the same grown-up look but provides a bit of heat. While these cheesy twists would overpower the oysters, they are perfect for dipping into hummus or tzatziki (see page 212). They also make a rich cracker replacement for when you're in the mood for soup or a bowl of chili. I've also been known to nibble them as is.

MAKES 48 | COMMITMENT LEVEL: DONE IN STAGES

2 teaspoons cumin seeds

2 teaspoons coriander seeds

1 teaspoon red-pepper flakes

1 cup unsalted butter, at room temperature

8 ounces cream cheese, at room temperature

1 clove garlic

2 cups all-purpose flour

1 teaspoon salt

1 egg

1 tablespoon water

1 cup grated Parmesan cheese

1. In a dry skillet over medium heat, toast the cumin, coriander, and pepper flakes until the seeds become fragrant and start to pop. Transfer to a blender, coffee grinder (reserved for spices only), or mortar and pestle and grind to a powder. Set aside.

2. Either by hand in a large bowl or in the bowl of a stand mixer fitted with a paddle, beat the butter and cream cheese until smooth. Place a microplane over the bowl and grate the garlic into the cream cheese mixture. Beat again to blend thoroughly.

3. In a medium bowl, whisk together the flour, salt, and reserved ground spice mixture. Add to the cream cheese mixture and blend until the dough comes together. Knead on a floured surface to combine. Cut the dough in half, flatten into disks, wrap in plastic wrap, and chill for 1 hour or overnight.

4. When ready to bake, preheat the oven to 350°F. Line 2 baking sheets with parchment paper. Remove 1 disk of dough from the refrigerator and let warm at room temperature for 10 minutes. Meanwhile, in a small bowl, whisk the egg and water together.

5. On a floured surface, roll the dough until it's $1/2$" thick. Sprinkle with 2 tablespoons of the cheese. Fold the dough in thirds, place seam side down, and roll again until it's $1/2$" thick. Sprinkle with another 2 tablespoons of the cheese, fold in thirds, place seam side down, and roll again to form a 6" × 8" rectangle. Cut into strips $1/4$" wide. Cut the strips in half so you have pieces of dough, each approximately $1/4$" × 4". (You can keep them 8" long if you wish, but short is easier to eat.)

6. Twist the end of each strip in opposite directions and place on the baking sheets about 1" apart. Brush with the egg mixture and sprinkle with 4 tablespoons of the cheese. While they are baking, roll the second batch.

7. Bake for 18 to 20 minutes, or until golden brown and baked all the way through. Serve hot from the oven.

NOTE: Twists will store in an airtight container for up to a week.

TIP: If you don't want to bake all the twists at one time, prepare them up to the point of baking. Freeze the unbaked twists on the baking sheet until solid. Once frozen, transfer the twists to a resealable freezer bag and return to the freezer. They'll keep for up to 2 months. When ready to bake, preheat the oven to 350°F, brush the twists with the egg wash, sprinkle with the Parmesan, and bake from frozen, adding 5 to 10 minutes to the baking time.

ROSEMARY AND BLACK OLIVE GRISSINI

These long, thin, crunchy breadsticks appeal to the child in me. I love how they snap when bitten and release their olive undertone. Even more, I love to play with them. Use them instead of a spoon to stir crème fraîche into your soup. Turn them into edible chopsticks and devour some roasted cauliflower (page 103), or challenge your fellow diners to a grissini duel. The winner gets all the breadsticks.

MAKES ABOUT 7 DOZEN | COMMITMENT LEVEL: DONE IN STAGES

1 cup warm water (about 110°F)

2½ cups bread flour

1 package (2¼ teaspoons) instant yeast

1 teaspoon fine sea salt

¼ cup black olive paste (see tip)

3 tablespoons minced fresh rosemary

NOTE: Grissini will keep in an airtight container for several days. Just keep the humidity away.

TIP: If you don't have black olive paste, you can make your own with pitted black olives such as kalamata, packed in oil. Remove the olives from the oil using a slotted spoon; place the olives in a blender and puree to a paste.

1. Either by hand in a large bowl or in the bowl of a stand mixer fitted with a dough hook, mix the water, flour, yeast, salt, olive paste, and rosemary. When the dough comes together, turn it onto a lightly floured surface and knead until smooth and elastic. The dough will be slightly oily because of the olive paste.

2. Transfer the dough to a lightly oiled bowl. Cover with plastic wrap and let stand at room temperature until doubled in volume (60 to 90 minutes).

3. Preheat the oven to 375°F. If your oven has a convection setting, place 3 racks in the oven and adjust the temperature according to your oven's requirements. Otherwise, place a rack in the center and bake 1 pan at a time. Line 4 baking sheets with parchment paper. If you don't have enough pans, cut at least 4 sheets of parchment so you have something to set the cut dough on.

4. On a lightly greased work surface, roll the dough to a rectangle about 20″ × 12″. The dough will be very easy to roll. Using a sharp knife or pizza cutter, cut the dough so you have strips that are 10″ long and ¼″ wide. Gently roll each breadstick beneath your palms to round the edges. If you like a twist in your breadstick, roll the ends in opposite directions.

5. Place the sticks on the baking sheets (or just on parchment paper if you don't have enough baking sheets) at least ¼″ apart. Cover with a tea towel and let rest for 30 minutes. Bake for 15 to 18 minutes, or until crisp and golden brown. Allow to cool on the baking sheets for a few minutes before transferring to racks to cool completely. Eat with soup, dip in tzatziki (page 212) or smoked paprika aioli (page 207), or just have as a snack by itself.

NOT-TOO-SPICY ROASTED CAULIFLOWER

If I had to eat cauliflower only one way for the rest of my life, I would ask for it to be roasted with spice. Roasting turns plain old one-note cauliflower into a nuanced, layered, and completely new vegetable. It's sweeter, more complex, slightly nutty, and totally beguiling. Would I get bored if handed a life sentence of roasted cauliflower? Never. I could scoop it up with crisp lavash bread (page 182), dunk it in citrusy Lime-Cilantro Dipping Sauce (page 204), or slip it quietly into Smoky Mushroom Crêpes (page 121). It would tire of me long before I tired of it.

MAKES 3 TO 4 SERVINGS | COMMITMENT LEVEL: READY IN AN HOUR OR LESS

1. Preheat the oven to 425°F. For even crispier results, use your oven's convection setting (if it has one) and adjust the temperature accordingly.

2. Place the cauliflower in a large bowl.

3. In a small bowl, whisk together the oil, chili powder, paprika, salt, and a good grinding of black pepper. Pour over the cauliflower florets and toss to thoroughly coat.

4. Spread the cauliflower in a single layer on a rimmed baking sheet and roast for 25 to 35 minutes, stirring after 15 minutes. The timing varies with the size of the pieces. You want the cauliflower to be deep golden and beginning to crisp. The tips of the stems might begin to blacken. Don't let them burn.

5. Serve the cauliflower hot with a squeeze of fresh lime juice (if using), Lime-Cilantro Dipping Sauce (page 204), or tzatziki of your choice (page 212).

NOTE: I have never had leftovers to store, because cauliflower shrinks substantially when roasted. If you do have leftovers, refrigerate them in an airtight container.

1 medium head cauliflower, cut into florets about 1½" wide (about 4 generous cups)

3 tablespoons vegetable oil

1 teaspoon chili powder

1 teaspoon smoked paprika

¼ teaspoon fine sea salt

Fresh ground black pepper

1 lime, cut into wedges (optional)

TIP: Cutting cauliflower into uniform pieces is key to even roasting. It sounds like a lot of work, but it's easy. First cut the head into quarters. Cut away the thickest part of the core. You can now pull the florets apart with your fingers or cut them with the tip of a paring knife.

CRISPY ROOT VEGETABLE CHIPS

This is an extremely flexible recipe. You can use the spice mix suggested, which is a blend of at least 15 Moroccan spices, or go as plain as salt and pepper. For something in between, try the spices used in Not-Too-Spicy Roasted Cauliflower (page 103).

*   A mandoline will reduce prep time considerably and allow for more consistent, thinner chips. If you don't have a mandoline, you can slice more thinly and consistently if you cut the vegetable in half, place the cut sides down, and then slice half-moon chips. Most food processor slicing disks aren't suitable, as they slice too thinly and the chips will burn.*

MAKES 4 SNACK SERVINGS | COMMITMENT LEVEL: READY IN AN HOUR OR LESS

1 pound root vegetables (potatoes, sweet potatoes, parsnips, turnips, taro, carrots, and/or beets)

3 tablespoons vegetable oil

4 teaspoons ras el hanout (available at Middle Eastern specialty shops)

1 teaspoon fine sea salt

NOTE: Once cooled, the chips can be stored in a resealable bag with the air squeezed out.

TIP: If you have an ovenproof rack, place it on the baking sheet, set the coated chips on the rack, and then bake. This eliminates the need to flip the chips.

1. Preheat the oven to 375°F. If your oven has a convection setting, use it and adjust the temperature accordingly. Line 3 baking sheets with parchment paper.

2. Wash the root vegetables. Leave the skin on or peel at your discretion. I leave the skin on for white potatoes but peel sweet potatoes. Slice the vegetables as thinly as you can. However, it's more important to be uniform than thin so that the chips bake evenly. Aim for $1/16''$ thick, but do not cut thicker than $1/8''$.

3. Place the slices on paper towels and blot dry. Arrange in a single layer on the baking sheets. Different vegetables bake at different rates, so if you are using a mix, arrange them 1 vegetable per pan.

4. In a small bowl, whisk together the oil, ras el hanout, and salt. Brush on the chips with a pastry brush. Flip the vegetables over and brush the oil mixture on the other side.

5. Bake for 10 minutes for $1/16''$ slices or 15 minutes for thicker slices. Remove the baking sheets from the oven, flip the chips over, and return the chips to a different rack for even cooking. Continue baking for 5 to 20 minutes, depending on how thick the chips are and what vegetable you're roasting. The chips are ready when they are golden and the edges curl or ruffle. The thinner the chip, the more pronounced the ruffle. (Keep an eye on the smaller chips because they cook faster.)

6. Transfer the chips to a layer of paper towels to cool. Eat as is, or dip in a tzatziki (page 212) or aioli variation (page 207) that suits your spice selection.

CHOCOLATE-TIPPED CIGARETTES

I don't smoke, but I do inhale the occasional tuile cigarette with my coffee. It is buttery like a shortbread, snaps like a fortune cookie, and has the sophisticated richness you expect from a French dessert. A hint of orange brightens the sweetness and plays well against the smoldering chocolate tip. Tuile cigarettes don't come with a warning label, but if they did, it might read: "Caution! May cause squeals of joy and increase risk of delight."

MAKES 15 TO 18 | COMMITMENT LEVEL: READY IN AN HOUR OR LESS

TUILES

1 cup sifted confectioners' sugar

$\frac{1}{2}$ teaspoon pure vanilla extract

3 egg whites

$\frac{1}{4}$ cup all-purpose flour

2 tablespoons ground almonds

$\frac{1}{4}$ cup melted unsalted butter

$1\frac{1}{2}$ teaspoons heavy cream

2 teaspoons finely grated orange peel

DIP

4 ounces dark chocolate, roughly
chopped

2 tablespoons butter

1 teaspoon orange liqueur (optional)

Ground almonds, for dusting (optional)

1. *To make the tuiles:* Preheat the oven to 400°F. Line baking sheets with parchment paper.

2. In a medium bowl, combine the confectioners' sugar, vanilla, and egg whites and whisk until smooth and foamy. Add the flour, almonds, butter, cream, and orange peel and mix well. The batter will be quite thin and liquid.

3. Drop 1 tablespoon of batter onto the baking sheet and spread with the back of a spoon to form an oval about 6" long and 3" wide. Form no more than 4 tuiles at a time, because otherwise they will cool before you can roll them. Bake for about 6 minutes, watching carefully to ensure they don't burn. The tuiles are done when the middles are light gold and the edges are dark gold.

4. Remove the baking sheet from the oven and let the tuiles sit for about 1 minute. Using a spatula and working quickly, gently lift 1 tuile at a time onto a flat surface and roll it around a bamboo skewer about $\frac{1}{8}$" in diameter. If you don't have a skewer, use the handle of a thin wooden spoon. Roll and place on parchment paper, seam side down so it won't unravel. Remove the skewer or wooden handle with a gentle twist and roll the next cookie. (Alternatively, you can drape tuiles over a rolling pin for a simple curve.) If the tuiles get too stiff, return them to the oven for 30 seconds. Repeat baking and rolling the remaining tuiles.

5. *To make the dip:* When all the tuiles have been rolled and are cooling, prepare the chocolate dip. Melt the chocolate and butter in a heatproof bowl over simmering (not boiling) water or in the microwave on medium power in

1-minute bursts. Stir in the orange liqueur, if using. Tipping the bowl to pool the chocolate, dip 1 end of a tuile cigarette into the chocolate about 1" to 2" deep. Hold over the almonds and sprinkle with the almonds before the chocolate dries, if using. Place the tuile on a sheet of parchment paper to set and repeat with the remaining tuiles.

NOTE: These are best eaten the same day and suffer greatly in humid conditions. If you have any leftovers, store them in an airtight container.

TIP: Even if you have only one baking sheet, you can speed things up. Scoop and shape all the tuiles on sheets of parchment paper before you start baking. When the pan comes out of the oven, remove the parchment paper with the hot cookies and replace it with a sheet of unbaked ones. The next pan of tuiles will bake while you roll.

DOUBLE-STUFF ÜBER-OREO COOKIES

This "Oreo" cookie is actually a classic pâte sablée pastry loaded with cocoa and acting as bookends for a decadent buttercream icing. I knew I nailed the recipe when a friend bit into one and giggled. She's not a giggler. Like the famous cookie that inspired it, this ultrarich chocolate treat with its double-thick middle pulls apart easily. While these cookies aren't a grab-a-handful after-school snack screaming for a glass of milk, they do gently request a second helping.

MAKES 36 TO 40 | COMMITMENT LEVEL: DONE IN STAGES

1. *To make the cookies:* Using an electric mixer or a stand mixer fitted with a paddle, beat the butter, confectioners' sugar, and salt together until light and fluffy. Add the yolks and vanilla and beat until soft and light.

2. Into a medium bowl, sift the flour and cocoa together. Using a large wooden spoon or the stand mixer on its lowest setting, blend the flour mixture into the butter mixture. When all of the flour mixture is incorporated, increase the speed to medium and beat to ensure the dough is well blended.

3. Divide the dough in half and spoon onto plastic wrap. Form each half into a roll 10" long and approximately 2" wide. Make the rolls as round as you can. If you can't make them uniformly round, make the rolls square. The aim is to be uniform, so pick the shape you can make best. Refrigerate for at least 2 hours or overnight. Alternatively, the raw dough can be frozen for a couple of months.

4. When you're ready to bake, preheat the oven to 325°F and line 2 baking sheets with parchment paper.

5. Using a sharp, thin-bladed knife, slice the dough into scant ¼"-thick rounds and place on the baking sheets about 1" apart. Bake for 15 to 18 minutes, or until the cookies are firm when touched in the middle. Cool on racks.

6. *To make the filling:* While the cookies are baking, prepare the filling. Using an electric mixer or a stand mixer fitted with a whisk, beat the butter until smooth. Add the confectioners' sugar, salt, and vanilla and beat on low speed to incorporate the sugar. When the sugar is fully

COOKIES

1½ cups unsalted butter, at room temperature

1½ cups sifted confectioners' sugar

½ teaspoon fine sea salt

2 egg yolks

1 tablespoon pure vanilla extract

1½ cups all-purpose flour

1½ cups Dutch-processed cocoa powder

FILLING

1 cup unsalted butter, at room temperature

3 cups sifted confectioners' sugar

Generous pinch of fine sea salt

2 teaspoons pure vanilla extract

(continued on page 110)

(continued from page 109)

absorbed, increase the speed and beat until the filling is very light. Keep beating. A bit more. This takes up to 5 minutes. You want the filling to be almost white.

7. To assemble, place 1 tablespoon of filling on the bottom of a cooled cookie, place a second cookie on top (bottom against the filling), and gently press. Repeat with the remaining cookies and filling.

NOTE: The cookies can be stored in an airtight container. Leftover filling can be frozen for the next time.

Variations: Feel free to play with the filling. Make it orange, coffee, mint, or any other chocolate-friendly flavor you like.

TIP: If you don't have Dutch-processed cocoa powder, use regular and add $\frac{1}{2}$ teaspoon baking soda.

ESPRESSO AND HAZELNUT BISCOTTI

To celebrate their 50th anniversary, my parents generously took the whole family on a group trip to Italy. For 10 days we toured, ate, laughed, and got hopelessly lost. I wanted to re-create our trip in cookie form. These espresso and hazelnut biscotti capture the essence of our time in Tuscany. Espresso powder is for the countless cups of cappuccino we drank in various piazzas, cinnamon for the dusting the barista put on them, hazelnuts for our Nutella binges, and a grating of orange for the unfailingly bright Florentine sky. The results? Delizioso.

MAKES ABOUT 4 DOZEN | COMMITMENT LEVEL: DONE IN STAGES

1½ cups hazelnuts

½ cup unsalted butter, at room temperature

1¼ cups sugar

Peel from 1 orange, finely grated

2 eggs at room temperature

1 tablespoon pure vanilla extract

2¾ cups all-purpose flour

1 teaspoon baking powder

1–1½ teaspoons cinnamon (optional)

1½ tablespoons instant espresso powder

½ cup dark chocolate chips

COATING (OPTIONAL)

8 ounces semisweet chocolate

¼ cup ground hazelnuts, for decoration

1. Preheat the oven to 350°F. Line a large baking sheet with parchment paper.

2. Once the oven comes up to heat, toast the hazelnuts in the oven on an unlined baking sheet for 10 minutes, or until fragrant. Turn the nuts out onto a clean tea towel and rub them to remove as much of the skin as possible. Roughly chop the nuts and set aside.

3. Using an electric mixer or a stand mixer with a paddle attachment, cream the butter, sugar, and orange peel until light and fluffy. Add the eggs and vanilla and beat until blended.

4. Into a large bowl, sift together the flour, baking powder, cinnamon (if using), and espresso powder. With the mixer on low or using a wooden spoon, mix the flour mixture into the butter mixture, stirring until just blended. Stir in the chocolate chips and reserved nuts.

5. Using floured hands, divide the dough in half and shape each half into a log about 12″ long. Place on the parchment-lined baking sheet and flatten to 1″ high. Bake for 25 to 35 minutes, or until the tops feel firm when lightly pressed. Remove the baking sheet from the oven, reduce the heat to 325°F, and let the logs cool for 15 minutes.

6. Transfer the logs to a cutting board. Using a serrated knife, cut each on the diagonal into slices about ½″ thick. Place the cookies cut side down on the parchment-lined baking sheet and bake for 10 minutes. Turn the cookies over and bake for 5 to 10 minutes, or until they start to brown. Transfer to a rack to cool.

7. *To make the coating* (if using): When the biscotti are cooled, gently melt the chocolate in a heatproof bowl over simmering, not boiling, water. Once melted, you can either drizzle the chocolate over the biscotti or dip half into the chocolate. See pages 29–31 for drizzling ideas. To dip, tip the bowl to pool the chocolate. Dip half of the cookie in the chocolate, place on a sheet of parchment paper, and dust with ground hazelnuts before the chocolate sets.

NOTE: Store between layers of parchment paper in an airtight container. Biscotti will keep for a couple of weeks.

TIP: Instant espresso is not the same as instant coffee. It's stronger and less harsh and doesn't have the metallic taste some instant coffees have. You can find instant espresso in the coffee section of some big chain supermarkets or in coffee shops. If you can't find it, use 2 heaping tablespoons of instant coffee.

CHEWY CRYSTALLIZED GINGER COOKIES

Each Christmas, every family member picks one type of cookie they'd like. Without so much as a second's hesitation, my husband asks for ginger cookies. Always. He adores the spicing and the sink-your-teeth-into-them chew. They are a perfect accompaniment to a steaming mug of hot apple cider. The crinkly tops don't hurt their cause. He has one stipulation: I must be the one who bakes them. Although the whole family uses this recipe, I am the only baker brave enough to pull them from the oven while still slightly underdone. Everyone else takes one look at the unfinished cookies and gives them an extra few minutes. Resist this urge. Early retrieval is the key to their ultrachewiness—and quite possibly the way to a chewy ginger cookie lover's heart.

MAKES ABOUT 3 DOZEN | COMMITMENT LEVEL: READY IN AN HOUR OR LESS

1. Position a rack in the center of the oven. Preheat the oven to 350°F.

2. In a large bowl, using either an electric mixer or a stand mixer fitted with a paddle, beat the butter and sugar until light and creamy. Beat in the egg and molasses.

3. In a separate bowl, combine the flour, baking soda, salt, ground ginger, cinnamon, and cloves. Add the crystallized ginger and mix lightly to coat with the flour mixture and distribute it evenly.

4. By hand or with the stand mixer on low, blend the flour mixture into the butter mixture.

5. Using a 1-tablespoon cookie scoop, place the dough on ungreased baking sheets. If you don't have a cookie scoop, use a spoon and then roll the dough into a ball. Place 2" apart to allow for spreading. If you want to get fancy, dip one side of the cookie in granulated sugar and place a small piece of crystallized ginger on top.

6. Bake 1 pan at a time in the middle of the oven for 8 to 10 minutes. Do not overbake. The cookies should be slightly undercooked when they come out of the oven. Leave on the pan for 2 minutes, or until they are solid enough to transfer to a rack.

NOTE: Once cooled, the cookies can be stored in an airtight container for up to a week or frozen for up to 2 months.

¾ cup salted butter, at room temperature

1 cup sugar, plus more for optional rolling

1 egg, at room temperature

¼ cup fancy molasses (not blackstrap)

2 cups all-purpose flour

2 teaspoons baking soda

¼ teaspoon fine sea salt

2 teaspoons ground ginger

1 teaspoon ground cinnamon

1 teaspoon ground cloves

½ cup finely chopped crystallized ginger, plus more for optional garnish

TIP: If you like orange with your ginger, add the finely grated peel of a large orange to the batter when you are beating the butter and sugar together.

SLOPPY

foods that drip or ooze their filling

Some food is so happy to be eaten, it literally jumps for joy. All over your fingers, the plate, your shirt, the table.

    If you want flavors that dance, avoid the food sitting all prim and proper with its ankles crossed neatly and its hands tucked into its lap. Instead, approach the empanada whose filling has shimmied onto the pan. Jive with the sandwich cookie that has more icing than biscuit. Rock the cream-jammed profiteroles. It takes two to tango. What are you waiting for?

SLOPPY

SAVORY

SWEET

SMOKY MUSHROOM CRÊPES

Crêpes make a cook look good. People think they're hard, but they're really just very thin pancakes with a fancy French name. Eating them—at least neatly—is more of a challenge than assembling them. This version combines some of my favorite flavors in an irresistible although sometimes sloppy filling. Meaty mushrooms, smoked paprika, and a swirl of decadent cream all come together in a satisfying dish that's rich but not too heavy.

MAKES 6 TO 8 | COMMITMENT LEVEL: READY IN AN HOUR OR LESS

1. *To make the crêpes:* In a blender, puree the milk, eggs, melted butter, flour, and salt until smooth. Set the batter aside at room temperature for 30 minutes to 1 hour. (You can make the crêpe batter the night before. Just cover with plastic wrap and refrigerate. Before cooking, allow the batter to come to room temperature.) While the batter rests, make the filling.

2. *To make the filling:* In a medium skillet over medium heat, heat the butter until it melts and bubbles. Cook the onion until soft and just beginning to turn golden. Add the garlic and cook for a minute or two. Add the smoked paprika, sweet paprika, and tomato paste and cook until the spices and tomato paste have blended with the onion. Add the mushrooms and salt and cook until the mushrooms are soft. Add the cream, sour cream, and lemon juice, stirring to make a thick sauce. Taste. Add more salt if needed and a good grinding of black pepper. Remove the pan from the heat. Cover it to keep the sauce warm while you cook the crêpes.

3. Heat an 8" nonstick skillet over medium-high heat. Brush with a bit of melted butter for the first crêpe. Pour 2 to 3 tablespoons of batter into the pan and tilt the pan in a circular motion so the batter covers the bottom in a thin layer. Cook for 45 to 60 seconds, or until the edge of the crêpe is brown and flecked with tiny bubbles and the middle looks dull. Turn and cook for 30 to 45 seconds. The second side should be cooked but will not be as dark as the first side. (Consider the first crêpe a trial run. They rarely work out, so don't panic. By the second or third, you should be turning like a pro.)

CRÊPES

½ cup milk

2 eggs, at room temperature

1 tablespoon melted unsalted butter, plus more for frying

½ cup all-purpose flour

Generous pinch of fine sea salt

FILLING

1 tablespoon unsalted butter

1 small onion, very finely chopped

1 clove garlic, grated on a microplane

½ teaspoon smoked paprika

1 teaspoon sweet paprika

2 tablespoons tomato paste

8 ounces sliced cremini mushrooms (about 4 cups)

¼ teaspoon fine sea salt, or more to taste

¼ cup heavy cream

¼ cup sour cream

1 tablespoon fresh lemon juice

Fresh ground black pepper

(continued on page 122)

(continued from page 121)

4. Place the crêpe flat on a plate. Scoop ¼ cup of the mushroom filling into its center and spread down the length of the crêpe. Fold the sides over the filling. Drizzle some filling sauce on top for show. Repeat with the remaining batter. You may or may not need to brush the pan again with butter for subsequent crêpes. Eat while hot.

NOTE: Unfilled leftover crêpes can be stored between sheets of waxed paper and refrigerated for up to 4 days. Reheat in a hot skillet for a few seconds, fill, fold, and enjoy. The filling can be refrigerated in an airtight container for up to 3 days.

TIP: Don't have a microplane? Then crush the clove of garlic and put "microplane" on your shopping list. It's worth the money and drawer space, as it can grate frozen ginger (see tip on page 62), zest citrus, turn block chocolate into fine shavings, and even grate hard cheeses like Parmesan.

CHICKEN, CORN, AND CILANTRO EMPANADAS

These are serendipity in a shell. I had fully intended to make cream cheese pastry and form the empanadas into traditional half-moons. But it was late, and I was tired, and there was leftover phyllo just begging to be used. So I tried a quick-fill version. Turns out people liked the package, so I'm passing the time-saving method onto you. No matter how you fold them, these empanadas are full of warm Mexican spices. Lime and cilantro give the mixture lift while corn adds sweetness. The chicken? She'd like to thank her amazing supporting cast for making her look so good.

MAKES 18 | COMMITMENT LEVEL: DONE IN STAGES

FILLING

3 tablespoons vegetable oil

2 onions, chopped

2 large cloves garlic, grated on
a microplane

2 teaspoons ground cumin

1 teaspoon ground coriander

2 canned chipotle chile peppers, minced

Peel of 2 limes, finely grated

1 cup finely chopped red bell pepper

1 cup corn, fresh or frozen and thawed

$\frac{1}{4}$ cup fresh lime juice

4 boneless, skinless chicken breasts,
cut into $\frac{1}{2}$" pieces (about 2 pounds)

$\frac{1}{4}$ teaspoon fine sea salt

8 ounces shredded Monterey Jack
cheese (about 2 cups)

1 cup packed chopped cilantro

2 eggs, lightly beaten

WRAPS

9 large sheets phyllo, defrosted

$\frac{1}{2}$ cup vegetable oil or melted butter

1. *To make the filling:* In a large skillet over medium heat, heat the oil. Cook the onions for 5 minutes, stirring occasionally, or until brown and soft. Add the garlic, cumin, coriander, chipotle peppers, and lime peel and cook for 1 minute. Add the bell pepper, corn, and lime juice and cook until the bell pepper softens.

2. Add the chicken and salt and cook until the chicken is no longer pink and the liquid has evaporated. Set aside to cool.

3. When you are ready to cook the empanadas, preheat the oven to 350°F. Set out two 12-cup muffin pans. Stir the cheese, cilantro, and eggs into the cooled chicken mixture, mixing to combine well.

4. *To make the wraps:* Lightly dampen a tea towel. Lay the phyllo sheets flat and place a damp tea towel on top of the stack to prevent the pastry from drying out. Remove 1 sheet at a time and, using a pastry brush, brush lightly with oil or melted butter. Place a second sheet on top of the first and brush with oil or butter. Repeat with a third sheet. Using a sharp knife, cut the phyllo stack into six 6" squares. Discard any excess trim. Place 1 square over a muffin cup and gently press the pastry into the cup, being careful not to tear it. Spoon $\frac{1}{4}$ cup of chicken filling into the cup. Fold the pastry flaps over the filling and press gently. Brush with more oil or butter. Repeat with the remaining ingredients. Bake for 20 to 25 minutes, or until the phyllo is golden and the filling is hot. Serve with Lime-Cilantro Dipping Sauce (page 204) or cilantro tzatziki (page 212), or enjoy as is.

NOTE: Leftovers will keep for 2 days in the refrigerator in an airtight container. Reheat in a 350°F oven for 10 to 15 minutes. Microwaving will make the phyllo soggy.

CHEDDAR TAPENADE ROLLS

This is my cousin Jude's favorite recipe in the book. If exclamation marks were currency and she were the bank, this recipe would have made me rich. The citrus lightens the saltiness of the olive-packed tapenade, the Cheddar adds bite, and the ricotta makes sure everything is smoothed out nicely. It's all wrapped in a phyllo shell that makes it a perfect appetizer or cocktail party snack.

MAKES 3 TO 4 DOZEN | COMMITMENT LEVEL: DONE IN STAGES

FILLING

1 cup tapenade (homemade or commercial)

Peel of 1 lemon or orange, finely grated

2 cups ricotta cheese

4 ounces finely grated aged Cheddar (about 1 cup)

2 eggs, at room temperature

WRAPS

1 package (1 pound) phyllo pastry, defrosted

½ cup vegetable oil or melted butter

> **TIP:** Any leftover filling makes a lovely addition to Crispy-Crust Pizza (page 156).

1. Preheat the oven to 375°F.

2. *To make the filling:* In a medium bowl, combine the tapenade, lemon or orange peel, ricotta, Cheddar, and eggs until well blended. If desired, the filling can be covered and refrigerated. Roll and bake within 3 days.

3. *To make the wraps:* Lightly dampen a tea towel. Lay the stack of phyllo sheets flat. Cut the stack in half crosswise. Stack the phyllo sheets on top of each other, remove 1 sheet, and place the damp towel on top of the stack to prevent the pastry from drying out.

4. Using a pastry brush, lightly brush the sheet with oil or butter. Spoon 1 heaping tablespoon of filling at the bottom of the sheet in the center. Roll the phyllo and filling toward the top of the sheet a few inches, up to halfway. When the filling is secure, fold the edges of the phyllo toward the center, covering the filling. You should use about a third of the sheet's width per side. Finish rolling the log. (If you want to roll a different shape, see pages 49–51 for rolling ideas.)

5. Place the tapenade roll seam side down on an ungreased baking sheet. Brush with more oil or butter. Continue making tapenade rolls until you run out of phyllo or filling. Bake for 12 minutes, or until golden brown and crispy. Serve hot.

NOTE: Leftovers can be refrigerated in an airtight container for up to 3 days. Reheat at 350°F for 10 minutes, or until hot all the way through. Do not reheat in the microwave. The pastry will become glue-like.

GINGER–CRUSTED STRAWBERRY MASCARPONE TART

Tiramisu is one of my favorite desserts. I love its velvety, sloppy texture and the irreplaceable richness only mascarpone can deliver. Unfortunately, it's been done so often, people roll their eyes when they hear its name. With summer berries coming at me fast and furious, I took the concept of the filling, skipped the alcohol, and made it a single layer. With ginger and lime added to the mix, this light, bright dessert is more lazy-patio than bustling-Italian-café. It's a bit soft and sloppy, just like its creator.

MAKES 6 TO 8 SERVINGS | COMMITMENT LEVEL: DONE IN STAGES

1. Preheat the oven to 350°F. Lightly butter a 10" flan pan.

2. *To make the crust:* In a blender or food processor, grind the cookies into crumbs. In a medium bowl, mix the cookie crumbs, brown sugar, and ginger together with a fork to combine. Drizzle the butter over the crumbs and mix until all of the crumbs are moistened. Firmly press the crumbs into the pan. Bake for 10 minutes. Let cool completely before filling.

3. *To make the filling:* In a large bowl using an electric mixer or the bowl of a stand mixer fitted with a whisk, beat the egg whites until soft peaks form. Set aside.

4. In a large bowl using an electric mixer or the bowl of a stand mixer fitted with a whisk, beat the yolks and granulated sugar for 5 minutes, or until pale and creamy and the sugar has dissolved. In a small bowl, using a spoon, blend the cheese, vanilla, and lime peel until smooth. Fold the cheese mixture into the yolk mixture. Add the reserved egg whites and fold gently. Spoon the filling into the crust.

5. Top with the strawberries. If using roasted berries, be sure to include their juice. Cover and refrigerate for at least 6 hours or overnight.

NOTE: The tart will keep for 2 days if covered and refrigerated, although the crust may become a bit soggy once the tart has been cut.

CRUST

2 cups ground ginger cookies (about 8 ounces whole)

2 tablespoons packed brown sugar

1 teaspoon ground ginger

¼ cup melted butter

FILLING

3 eggs, separated

6 tablespoons granulated sugar

1 container (8.8 ounces) mascarpone cheese (1 generous cup)

1 teaspoon vanilla bean paste (or pure vanilla extract)

Peel of 1 lime, finely grated

1 cup sliced strawberries or 1 recipe Balsamic Roasted Strawberries (page 215)

TIP: When a recipe calls for beating egg yolks and egg whites separately, whip the whites first to avoid inadvertently getting yolk in the whites. The whisk attachment on my stand mixer is a master at hiding specks of yolk and has ruined more than one batch of egg whites.

EXTRA-CRISPY PEACH AND BLUEBERRY CRISP

I had made some zucchini fries using panko and, being a very messy baker, hadn't cleaned up fully from the night before. When I was creating this recipe, I saw the panko crumbs, which are extremely crisp, and thought, "Crisp for the crisp." Unlike traditional crumb toppings made from oats or flour, this one is extra crunchy, in perfect contrast to the tender, classic summertime blueberry-and-peach mixture bubbling away beneath the surface. To enjoy the topping at its crunchiest, eat the crisp while still warm from the oven, but be careful when you serve it. The juices like to slop about.

MAKES 6 TO 8 SERVINGS | COMMITMENT LEVEL: READY IN AN HOUR OR LESS

FILLING

½ cup lightly packed brown sugar

1 tablespoon cornstarch

Peel of 1 orange, finely grated

3 cups pitted, peeled, and chopped peaches

4 cups blueberries

1 teaspoon pure vanilla extract

TOPPING

1 ½ cups panko bread crumbs

½ cup lightly packed brown sugar

½ cup chopped hazelnuts

¼ teaspoon fine sea salt

⅓ cup melted unsalted butter

NOTE: This dessert is best eaten the day it's made. Any leftovers should be covered and refrigerated. Soggy topping can be rescued with a minute under the broiler.

1. Preheat the oven to 350°F.

2. *To make the filling:* In a small bowl, mix the brown sugar, cornstarch, and orange peel until evenly combined.

3. In a large bowl, place the peaches and blueberries. Sprinkle with the vanilla and toss gently to evenly distribute the fruit. Sprinkle with the sugar mixture and toss gently to coat evenly. Spoon into an 8″ × 8″ glass baking dish. Level with the back of the spoon.

4. *To make the topping:* In a medium bowl, toss the panko, brown sugar, hazelnuts, and salt until well combined. Pour the butter over the crumbs and toss to coat well. Spoon the crumbs evenly over the fruit. Bake for 40 to 45 minutes, or until the fruit is bubbling and the topping is crispy. Allow to cool for 30 to 45 minutes before serving. The crisp can be served warm or at room temperature. Eat as is or topped with Chantilly Cream (page 135), ice cream, crème anglaise (page 222), or crème fraîche (page 224).

TIP: Crisps are a great way to use up fruit that is almost past its prime. Be sure to remove bruises before chopping. For best results, try to cut the fruit into uniform pieces. Panko are coarse, extra-crispy bread crumbs often used in Japanese cooking. Once confined to Asian markets, these crumbs can now be found in most large chain grocery stores. Look in the Asian section or in the regular bread crumbs/melba toast aisle.

BOOZY CHOCOLATE TORTE

Talk about versatile: This cake can take almost any chocolate-friendly pairing you throw at it—orange, cherry, raspberry. Don't like fruit? Try rum and the Boozy Brown Sugar Whipped Cream on page 218. Making it for Christmas? Get festive with chopped-up candy canes and crème de menthe. The cocoa gives the chocolate depth, but if you want a subtler backdrop, omit the cocoa powder and add $1/4$ cup more flour. The result will be a moderately light but fairly thirsty cake, ready and willing to soak up all the liqueur, fruit, and whipped cream you place between its eager layers. If done right, it will act a little drunk, staggering sloppily to the plate when you serve it.

MAKES 10 TO 12 SERVINGS | COMMITMENT LEVEL: DONE IN STAGES

1. Preheat the oven to 350°F. Grease two 9" round pans and line with parchment paper.

2. *To make the cake:* In a large heatproof bowl, combine the chocolate and butter. Microwave on low power or set over a pot of simmering water to gently melt. Stir the chocolate and butter together with a spoon. Add the granulated sugar, milk, flour, cocoa, baking powder, salt, eggs, and vanilla at once, beating until smooth.

3. Pour the batter into the pans, making the cakes as even as possible. If you have a kitchen scale, the easiest way to do this is to weigh the pans. Push the batter to the edges of the pan so the cake will remain relatively flat when it rises during baking. Bake for 30 minutes, or until a wooden pick inserted in the center comes out clean. Allow the cakes to cool for 10 to 15 minutes. Turn out of the pans onto wire racks, remove the parchment paper, and allow to cool to room temperature.

4. Slice each cake in half horizontally. (See the tip on page 133) for easy ways to do this.)

5. *To make the filling:* In a large bowl, using an electric mixer on high speed, beat the cream with the confectioners' sugar until soft peaks form.

6. Place 1 layer of cake on the platter or stand you will be serving it on. Drizzle with about one-quarter of the liqueur. Spread with one-quarter of the whipped cream, leaving a $1/4$" edge of cake showing. The weight of the cake will push the cream to the sides. Dot with one-quarter of

CAKE

4 ounces unsweetened chocolate, chopped

1 cup unsalted butter

2 cups granulated sugar

1 cup milk, at room temperature

$1 1/4$ cups all-purpose flour

$1/4$ cup sifted Dutch-processed cocoa powder

4 teaspoons baking powder

1 teaspoon fine sea salt

4 eggs, at room temperature

2 teaspoons pure vanilla extract

FILLING

2 cups heavy cream

3 tablespoons confectioners' sugar

$1/2$ cup (or more) liqueur of choice (such as orange, chocolate, raspberry, coffee, cherry, or hazelnut)

1 cup fruit, nuts, or other matching flavor item of choice

1 ounce semisweet chocolate, grated

(continued on page 133)

(continued from page 131)

the fruit/nuts/filling of choice and sprinkle with one-quarter of the grated chocolate. Repeat with the remaining layers of cake, whipped cream, fruit/nuts/filling, and chocolate.

7. Cover and refrigerate for at least 2 hours or overnight. Serve carefully; this is a very messy cake and can fall apart en route to the plate.

NOTE: Leftover cake can be wrapped in plastic wrap and stored in the refrigerator for up to 3 days. It also freezes well for up to a month.

TIP: You can use a serrated knife, but the easiest way to slice a cake in half horizontally is with thread or unflavored dental floss. Just wrap a length of thread around the sides of the cake where you want the cut to be made. Cross the ends of the thread and pull them gently but firmly away from each other. The thread will cut through the cake as you pull.

PROFITEROLES

Choux is the rebel of pastries. It's made on the stove top, not in a bowl, and bites its proverbial thumb at the standard pastry rules that have you cutting in cold butter and mollycoddling the dough as if it were a newborn. With choux pastry, melted butter, heat, and a good stiff beating are key. The resulting dough is a thick paste you can scoop, drop, or pipe. And once baked? You get a pastry studded with air pockets, just ready and willing to hold all the cream you can pipe into it. Yeah, it's a rebel, but with a deliciously drippy cause—cream.

MAKES ABOUT 3 DOZEN | COMMITMENT LEVEL: DONE IN STAGES

1. Preheat the oven to 375°F. Line 2 baking sheets with parchment paper.

2. *To make the choux pastry:* In a heavy saucepan over medium-high heat, combine the butter, granulated sugar, salt, milk, and water. Heat until the mixture just begins to boil. Reduce the heat to low and dump all the flour into the pan. With a wooden spoon or heat-resistant spatula, stir until the dough forms a ball.

3. Place the dough in the bowl of a food processor fitted with a steel blade. Pulse once or twice. With the food processor running, add the 4 eggs, one at a time, until combined. Alternatively, you can beat in the eggs one at a time by hand or with an electric mixer. The dough should be smooth and shiny and hold its shape.

4. Drop the dough onto the baking sheets to create profiteroles. You can do this using a pastry bag fitted with a large plain tip, a 1-tablespoon cookie scoop, or 2 dessert spoons. The aim is to make balls of dough about 1½" wide and tall so that filling them is easier. Regardless of the size you create, be consistent so they bake at the same rate. When all the profiteroles have been formed, tap down their points with a clean finger dipped in cold water.

5. In a small bowl, whisk the yolk with the cream or milk. Brush each profiterole with the egg wash. Bake for 20 to 25 minutes, or until the profiteroles are golden brown. Allow to cool completely before filling.

6. *To make the chantilly cream:* In a large bowl, using an electric mixer on high speed, beat the cream,

CHOUX PASTRY

½ cup unsalted butter

2 tablespoons granulated sugar

½ teaspoon fine sea salt

½ cup milk

½ cup water

1¼ cups all-purpose flour

4 eggs, at room temperature

1 egg yolk plus 1 tablespoon heavy cream or milk (for glazing)

CHANTILLY CREAM

2 cups heavy cream, cold

¼ cup confectioners' sugar

1 teaspoon pure vanilla extract

(continued on page 136)

(continued from page 135)

confectioners' sugar, and vanilla until soft peaks form. Fill the profiteroles immediately.

7. *To fill the profiteroles with a tip:* Put the cream into a pastry bag fitted with a small tip. Using a skewer, poke a hole in the side of the profiterole, insert the piping bag tip into the hole, and fill until you feel resistance. Repeat with the remaining profiteroles and cream.

   To fill the profiteroles without a tip: Using a serrated knife, cut the profiteroles in half horizontally, spoon a dollop of cream onto the bottoms, and then place the tops on gently.

8. Chill the filled profiteroles until ready to serve. Profiteroles can be served as is or drizzled with Chocolate Anything Sauce (see page 216). Salted Caramel Sauce (page 220) or Nutmeg Brandy Sauce (page 221) makes a nice change of pace.

NOTE: Any uneaten, sauce-free profiteroles can be refrigerated in an airtight container for up to 3 days.

TIP: You can use regular or confectioners' sugar for the chantilly cream, but confectioners' sugar adds a bit of structure and makes the cream a bit easier to handle.

RASPBERRY BUTTER TARTS

Pop into a Canadian bakery and you'll see a range of butter tarts for sale. Look in any cook's recipe box and you'll find a family butter tart recipe or two. Or three. We bakers like to outdo ourselves with creative variations. Classics are studded with raisins, coconut, or walnuts. Modern takes include chocolate chunks, toffee bits, and peanut butter chips. I've yet to see a raspberry version and can't figure out why. Tangy raspberries so perfectly balance the sweet, sweet filling that I may never go back to the classic form again. If you fall for these like I have, say you saw it here first.

MAKES APPROXIMATELY 2 DOZEN | COMMITMENT LEVEL: READY IN AN HOUR OR LESS

1 recipe No-Fail Pastry (Lard or Shortening Version) (page 45)

2 eggs, at room temperature

2 cups packed brown sugar

2 tablespoons fresh lemon juice

1 teaspoon pure vanilla extract

$1/2$ cup melted salted butter

Whole raspberries, fresh or frozen and not thawed, 3–4 per tart, depending on size

Whipped cream and additional raspberries, for garnish (optional)

TIP: Want to make only a small batch? Go ahead. The leftover filling—without the berries—freezes really well. Just defrost it, mix, and then pour it over the berry-filled shells and bake.

1. Preheat the oven to 400°F. Grease two 12-cup muffin pans or twenty-four $2 1/2$" disposable tart pans.

2. On a floured surface, roll the pie dough to $1/8$" thick. Using a $3 1/2$" cookie cutter or a clean, empty 19-ounce can, cut 24 rounds. Gently press the cut dough into the muffin pans or tart pans placed on a baking sheet. Chill until ready to use.

3. In a small bowl, whisk together the eggs, brown sugar, lemon juice, vanilla, and butter.

4. Place 3 or 4 raspberries in the bottom of each tart shell. Spoon the filling over the berries, filling the shell only two-thirds full. Any fuller and the filling will overflow, making it impossible to remove the tart without damaging the dessert or your ego.

5. Bake for 20 minutes, or until the crusts are golden and the filling is bubbly. Place the pans on a rack to cool. Allow the tarts to cool fully before removing from the pans with a nonserrated knife. Serve as is or with a dollop of whipped cream and a raspberry on top, if using.

NOTE: Store the tarts in the refrigerator in an airtight container for up to 5 days. These tarts can be frozen, but the crust will likely suffer a bit due to the filling's high sugar content.

CITRUS AND SPICE CRÊPES

Inspired by the classic crêpes suzette, this sauce provides a hit of orange without the need to flambé. The crêpes are tender and unassuming, and the filling delivers a familiar citrus flavor with an exotic hint of warm spices. I've kept the potentially aggressive star anise in check, but the orange needs some form of cream to tone it down.

MAKES 12 TO 16 | COMMITMENT LEVEL: DONE IN STAGES

1. *To make the crêpes:* In a small bowl, whisk together the milk, eggs, melted butter, and vanilla.

2. In a medium bowl, combine the flour, salt, and granulated or vanilla sugar. Gradually whisk the milk mixture into the flour mixture. The batter will be the consistency of table cream. Let rest at room temperature for 30 minutes. (You can make the batter the night before. Just cover with plastic wrap and refrigerate. Allow the batter to come to room temperature before cooking.)

3. *To make the citrus sauce:* While the crêpe batter rests, make the sauce. Wash and dry the oranges. With a vegetable peeler, cut long, shallow strips of peel from the oranges, being careful to avoid the bitter white pith. Segment the oranges (see tip on page 140) and place in a large skillet. Squeeze any remaining juices over the orange segments. Add the strips of orange peel, lemon juice, honey, vanilla bean, cinnamon, ginger, and star anise. Bring the mixture to a boil over medium-high heat. Boil for 15 minutes, or until the sauce begins to thicken. Using a slotted spoon or fork, remove the orange peel, vanilla bean, cinnamon, ginger, and star anise. Stir in the butter, liqueur (if using), and salt. Set aside until you are ready to fill the crêpes.

4. Once the batter has rested, heat an 8" nonstick skillet over medium heat. Brush with a bit of melted butter for the first crêpe. Pour 2 to 3 tablespoons of batter into the pan and tilt the pan in a circular motion so the batter covers the bottom in a thin layer. Cook for 45 to 60 seconds, or until the edge of the crêpe is brown and flecked with tiny bubbles and the middle looks dull. Turn the crêpe and cook for 30 to 45 seconds. The second side should be cooked but will not be as dark as the first side.

(continued on page 140)

CRÊPES

1 cup 2% or whole milk, at room temperature

3 eggs, at room temperature

2 tablespoons melted unsalted butter, plus more for frying

1 tablespoon pure vanilla extract

1 cup all-purpose flour

$\frac{1}{8}$ teaspoon fine sea salt

1 tablespoon granulated sugar or vanilla sugar (page 39)

CITRUS SAUCE

3 navel oranges

2 tablespoons fresh lemon juice

$\frac{1}{2}$ cup honey

$\frac{1}{2}$ vanilla bean, split lengthwise

1 stick (3") cinnamon

4 slices (1" each) fresh ginger

1 star anise

2 tablespoons unsalted butter

2 tablespoons orange liqueur (optional)

Pinch of fine sea salt

TOPPING

Crème fraîche (page 224), crème anglaise (page 222), or vanilla ice cream

Confectioners' sugar, for sprinkling

(continued from page 139)

(Consider the first a test crêpe. By the second or third, you will be turning like a pro.)

5. Place the crêpe pale side up on a plate. Fold it in half and then in half again to form a wedge. Add a dollop of crème fraîche, crème anglaise, or vanilla ice cream. Spoon some of the citrus sauce over the crêpe, being sure to get a few orange segments along with the liquid. Dust with confectioners' sugar and serve. Repeat with the remaining batter. You may or may not need to brush the pan again with butter for subsequent crêpes.

NOTE: Plain leftover crêpes can be stored between sheets of waxed paper and refrigerated for up to 4 days. Reheat in a hot skillet for a few seconds, fold, top, and enjoy.

TIP: To segment the oranges easily, cut them in half around the middle. Using a grapefruit or paring knife, cut each segment from the rind, then from its adjoining orange segment. Scoop the orange segments out with a small spoon.

RASPBERRY-STUFFED FRENCH TOAST

The thought of tossing leftover brioche brings tears to my eyes. I can't bear to see past-its-prime challah fed to the birds or dried-out panettone tossed to the squirrels. To save the specialty bread and my sanity, I found a way of restoring its former glory, thanks to an upscale twist on a familiar recipe. With a rich, berry-studded cream filling, this stuffed French toast is worthy of a Mother's Day brunch or holiday breakfast. The rich berry-and-cream filling will spill a bit when you eat, but that just shows it's full of melty goodness. For an over-the-top treat, use leftover sticky buns (page 165)—if you have any left.

MAKES 4 SERVINGS | COMMITMENT LEVEL: READY IN AN HOUR OR LESS

1. If your skillet won't hold 4 slices of bread at once, preheat the oven to 250°F for warming.

2. *To make the filling:* In the bowl of a stand mixer fitted with a paddle or in a medium bowl using an electric mixer, beat the mascarpone and cream cheeses at medium speed until well blended. Add the orange peel, granulated sugar, and vanilla and beat until well blended. Beat in the raspberries until they are broken up and distributed but not badly smashed. Set the filling aside. If you are making the filling ahead of time, cover it with plastic wrap and refrigerate. Bring to room temperature before using.

3. *To make the French toast:* In a medium bowl, whisk the eggs, milk, cream, vanilla, and cinnamon. Pour into a pie plate for easy dipping.

4. Spread one-quarter of the reserved filling on a slice of bread. Place a second slice on top and press together gently. Assemble the remaining 3 servings of French toast.

5. In a large skillet or electric frying pan, melt the butter over medium heat until foamy. Working quickly, dip the stuffed French toast in the egg mixture and turn quickly to coat the other side. Immediately place it gently in the skillet or electric frying pan so as not to spill the filling. Fry each piece of stuffed French toast for 4 to 6 minutes, turning once, or until golden. (If you can't cook all the French toast sandwiches in the same pan at once, cook them in batches and keep the finished ones warm in the oven until you're ready to serve.)

6. Slice the French toast sandwiches in half diagonally and

(continued on page 143)

FILLING

½ cup mascarpone cheese

¼ cup cream cheese

Peel of 1 orange (about 2 tablespoons)

2 tablespoons granulated sugar

½ teaspoon pure vanilla extract

1 cup fresh or frozen and thawed raspberries

FRENCH TOAST

3 eggs, at room temperature

¼ cup 2% or whole milk

¼ cup heavy cream

1 teaspoon pure vanilla extract

⅛ teaspoon ground cinnamon

8 slices rich specialty bread (such as brioche, panettone, or challah), sliced ½" thick

2 tablespoons butter

Raspberries, confectioners' sugar, maple syrup, Berry Sauce (page 223), or Boozy Brown Sugar Whipped Cream made with raspberry liqueur (page 218)

(continued from page 141)

serve hot, sprinkled with a few berries and the topping of your choice.

NOTE: Leftovers can be wrapped and refrigerated for a couple of days. Bring to room temperature and fry in a nonstick skillet over medium-low heat until heated through and sizzling. Microwaving will just produce a soggy sandwich. If you have filling left over, store it in an airtight container and use within 2 days.

TIP: Work quickly when dipping bread for French toast. While bread pudding needs to sit awhile and soak up the custard, soggy bread just makes for gooey French toast. And not the good kind of gooey.

SMUDGY

food that makes you wipe your face

In my kitchen, sticky buns lead to sticky fingers. Pizza, waffles, fritters, and pie all leave smudgy forensic evidence of what I have eaten and where.

If I had a time machine, I'd go back and secure the patent for the disposable paper napkin. Not only would I be rich, but with an endless supply at my fingertips, my clothes would remain stain free and I'd be able to sneak a Chocolate-Orange Gingersnap Drop without being given away by a telltale smear. Or two.

SMUDGY

BACON, CHEDDAR, AND THYME WAFFLES

I struggle as a short-order cook. My over-easy eggs always break. I can never get the yolk right with poached eggs. By the time the family is fed, I'm totally scrambled and anything but sunny-side up. My solution? Waffles. Fluffy, everyone-gets-the-same waffles. This savory version rolls three breakfast foods into one. Bacon, waffles, and cheese combine for a smoke-kissed treat that needs only a touch of sour cream and a drizzle of pure maple syrup. The eggs still make an appearance, but the whites are beaten and folded into the batter to keep the waffles as light as my mood.

MAKES 8 | COMMITMENT LEVEL: READY IN AN HOUR OR LESS

¾ cup all-purpose flour

¼ cup cornstarch

½ teaspoon baking powder

½ teaspoon baking soda

¼ teaspoon fine sea salt (optional, depending on how salty your bacon is)

2 tablespoons packed dark brown sugar

¼ teaspoon fresh ground black pepper (optional)

8 slices crisply cooked bacon, broken into ¼" pieces (¾ cup)

2 ounces shredded aged Cheddar cheese (about ½ cup)

1 tablespoon minced fresh thyme

2 eggs, separated

¼ cup melted unsalted butter

1 cup buttermilk

Sour cream, for garnish

Pure maple syrup, for garnish

1. Preheat your waffle iron.

2. In a large bowl, whisk together the flour, cornstarch, baking powder, baking soda, salt, brown sugar, and pepper (if using). Add the bacon, cheese, and thyme, tossing to coat well with the flour mixture.

3. In a medium bowl, combine the egg yolks, butter, and buttermilk. Whisk to combine well.

4. In a medium bowl, using an electric mixer on high speed, beat the egg whites until soft peaks form. Do not overwhip.

5. Add the buttermilk mixture to the flour mixture and stir until moist. Gently fold in the whipped egg whites. Spoon the batter into the hot waffle iron and cook according to the manufacturer's directions. The amount of batter and cooking time will vary with the model of the waffle iron.

6. Serve the hot waffles immediately, topped with your favorite breakfast eggs or with a dollop of sour cream and a drizzle of maple syrup for a decadent brunch.

7. Leftover waffles can be stored in an airtight container in the refrigerator or frozen. They can be brought back (almost) to their former glory by warming to room temperature and then being popped into a toaster or back into a hot waffle iron.

TIP: Want an even more indulgent version? Use Caramelized Bacon (page 82) instead of regular cooked bacon and top with crème fraîche (page 224) instead of sour cream.

PEPPERY PEAR AND SMOKED GOUDA DUTCH BABY

If a popover and a pancake got together for a romantic tryst, the result would be a bouncing Dutch baby. Like a popover, this dish emerges from the oven puffed and light and proud as punch. Ooh and ahh quickly, as this baby takes on the features of its pancake parentage within minutes. In this version, a layer of peppery sautéed pears naps beneath a blanket of smoked Gouda batter.

MAKES 4 TO 6 SERVINGS | COMMITMENT LEVEL: READY IN AN HOUR OR LESS

1. Place a rack in the center of the oven and a heavy 10″ skillet on the rack to heat. Cast iron is ideal, but any oven-proof skillet will do. Preheat the oven to 425°F.

2. In a medium bowl, whisk the milk, eggs, and melted butter until smooth. Add the flour, cornstarch, and salt. Whisk until smooth. Grate the cheese using the large holes of a box grater. Add it to the batter and stir gently to combine. Set aside while you cook the pears.

3. Peel, core, and cut the pears into ¼″-thick slices. In a large skillet over medium heat, melt the room-temperature butter. When it bubbles, place the pears in the butter, add a light grinding of pepper, and cook, stirring often, for 4 to 5 minutes, or until the pears are lightly golden and beginning to get tender.

4. When the pears are done, remove the heated skillet from the oven. Slide the pears into the hot skillet and arrange in a single layer. Be sure to scrape out all the butter. Give the reserved batter a quick stir, pour it over the pears, and pop the skillet back into the oven. Bake for 15 to 20 minutes, or until puffed and golden. The Dutch baby will not rise as high as a plain version because of the cheese. This is normal. You didn't do anything wrong.

5. Slice and serve with a dollop of crème fraîche (page 224) or sour cream, a grinding of fresh black pepper, and a drizzle of honey.

NOTE: Dutch babies don't sleep well. Eat this dish hot from the oven. Technically, leftovers can be stored in the refrigerator in an airtight container and reheated in a skillet, but they might disappoint. If this is the case, serve with Caramelized Bacon (page 82) to take the edge off.

1 cup milk

3 eggs, at room temperature

2 tablespoons melted unsalted butter

¾ cup all-purpose flour

¼ cup cornstarch

½ teaspoon fine sea salt

4 ounces smoked Gouda

2 pears (such as Bosc)

2 tablespoons unsalted butter, at room temperature

Fresh cracked black pepper

Crème fraîche or sour cream, for garnish

Honey, for drizzling

TIP: If you don't have smoked Gouda, this recipe works with aged Gouda. Don't like Gouda? Substitute Edam or smoked Cheddar.

DILL ZUCCHINI FRITTERS WITH LEMON TZATZIKI

One year I planted too many zucchini. They arrived nonstop all summer. We pureed them into soup. Grated them into breads and muffins. We diced, we sliced, we even julienne fried. These fritters come from one of the recipes I developed in self-defense, and it turned out to be one of my favorite summer recipes. Zucchini might be pushy in the garden, but it's gracious when introduced to fresh herbs and feta. It also looks rather natty with a tzatziki hat. Should the Zucchini Apocalypse beat down your kitchen door, invite the gang in, and then pull out the grater and the frying pan. Survival never tasted so good.

MAKES 8 | COMMITMENT LEVEL: READY IN AN HOUR OR LESS

LEMON TZATZIKI

1/2 cup Greek yogurt

1 clove garlic

1/4 teaspoon fine sea salt

Fresh ground black pepper

1 tablespoon minced fresh dill

3 sprigs fresh mint, minced

Peel of 1/2 lemon, finely grated

1 tablespoon fresh lemon juice

FRITTERS

2 cups grated zucchini (about 2 small;
   see grating instructions in Step 2)

3/4 cup all-purpose flour

1 teaspoon baking powder

1/2 teaspoon fine sea salt

1/2 teaspoon fresh cracked black
   pepper, plus more for garnish

1 tablespoon minced fresh mint leaves

2 tablespoons minced fresh dill

1 large clove garlic

1 egg, at room temperature

Peel of 1 lemon, finely grated

2 tablespoons fresh lemon juice

6 tablespoons water

1 small onion, very finely chopped

4 ounces feta cheese, crumbled

2 tablespoons vegetable oil

1. *To make the Lemon Tzatziki:* In a medium bowl, stir the yogurt until smooth. Using a microplane, mince the garlic into the yogurt. Add the salt, pepper, dill, mint, lemon peel, and lemon juice. Stir and taste, adding more salt if needed. Cover and refrigerate until ready to use. This can be made ahead of time; it tastes better if allowed to mellow overnight. Tzatziki will keep in the refrigerator for up to 1 week.

2. *To make the fritters:* Wash and cut the zucchini in half lengthwise. If the zucchini is large, remove the seeds with a spoon or melon baller. Using the large holes of a box grater, grate the zucchini and set in a mesh strainer or colander to drain.

3. In a large bowl, whisk the flour, baking powder, salt, pepper, mint, and dill.

4. Using a microplane, grate the garlic into a small bowl. Add the egg, lemon peel, lemon juice, and water and beat with a fork to combine. Pour over the flour mixture and stir to combine. Stir in the onion, cheese, and drained zucchini.

(continued on page 154)

(continued from page 152)

5. In a large nonstick skillet over medium heat, heat 1 table-spoon of the oil. Using a cookie scoop or spoon, drop $1/4$ cup of batter per fritter into the pan and flatten to $3/4''$ thick. Add additional batter for fritters as you are able without crowding the pan. Cook about 6 minutes, turning once, or until golden brown and cooked through. Repeat with the remaining batter, using more oil as needed. Serve hot with a dollop of Lemon Tzatziki and fresh ground black pepper.

NOTE: Fritters are best eaten hot. Any leftovers can be stored in the refrigerator for up to 3 days and reheated in a skillet.

TIP: If you can't find Greek yogurt, you can make your own with standard plain yogurt. Place a strainer lined with two or three basket-shaped coffee filters or several layers of cheesecloth over a bowl. Empty a tub of plain yogurt into it, cover with plastic wrap, and set in the refrigerator for several hours or even overnight to drain. The yogurt will be reduced by at least half. Discard the yogurt water and use the strained yogurt in tzatziki.

SMOKED PAPRIKA CORN FRITTERS

I love corn so much that eating it one way just isn't enough. These spiced fritters can be fried in a pan or cooked in a waffle iron. The fried version highlights the corn taste, while the waffle version provides contrast with a crunchy outside, soft inside. Either way, once topped with a dollop of sour cream, a sprinkle of cilantro, and some fresh lime juice, these corn-filled cakes will leave you wiping your mouth and asking for seconds.

MAKES 8 TO 10 FRITTERS OR 2 OR 3 LARGE WAFFLES | COMMITMENT LEVEL: READY IN AN HOUR OR LESS

1. In a large bowl, whisk the flour, baking powder, salt, paprika, coriander, cumin, red pepper (if using), cilantro, and lime peel.

2. Using a microplane, grate the garlic into a small bowl. Add the egg, lime juice, and water and beat with a fork to combine. Pour over the flour mixture and stir to combine. Stir in the corn.

3. *Pan-frying method:* In a large nonstick skillet over medium heat, heat 1 tablespoon of the oil. Using a large cookie scoop or spoon, drop ¼ cup of batter into the pan and flatten to ¾" thick. Add additional batter for fritters as you are able without crowding the pan. Cook for 6 minutes, turning once, or until golden brown and cooked through. Repeat with the remaining batter, using more oil as needed.

   Waffle iron method: Heat and oil a waffle iron according to the manufacturer's instructions. Cook the batter in the heated waffle iron, following the manufacturer's instructions for batter quantity and timing.

4. Serve hot with a dollop of sour cream, a squeeze of fresh lime juice, and a sprinkle of cilantro.

TIP: Unless it's of great sentimental value, toss your garlic press and replace it with a microplane. Anytime a recipe calls for crushed garlic, grab the microplane instead. This method releases more flavor, requires almost no strength (which is ideal if you have arthritis), and makes for a quick cleanup.

¾ cup all-purpose flour

1 teaspoon baking powder

½ teaspoon fine sea salt

1 teaspoon smoked paprika

1 teaspoon ground coriander

1 tablespoon ground cumin

⅛ teaspoon ground red pepper (optional)

¼ cup minced cilantro

Peel of 1 lime, finely grated

1 clove garlic

1 egg

2 tablespoons fresh lime juice

6 tablespoons water

2 cups corn, fresh off the cob or frozen and thawed

2 tablespoons vegetable oil

Sour cream, fresh lime juice, and additional minced cilantro, for garnish

NOTE: No matter which cooking method you use, these are best eaten the day they are made.

CRISPY-CRUST PIZZA WITH FIVE VARIATIONS

We tend to think of pizza as a fast food, but the secret to an authentic thin-crust Italian pizza is slow-rising dough—very slow rising. Almost glacially slow. This recipe is inspired by the no-knead pizza dough developed by Jim Lahey, owner of Sullivan St. Bakery in New York City. It's thin, light, very crisp, and edged with bubbles. While this dough tastes best when given a 24-hour head start, it takes only about 5 minutes to cook to crispy perfection. If you like your pizza thick and chewy, use focaccia dough (page 76). But for a taste of true Italy, plan ahead and go easy on the toppings.

MAKES FOUR 10" TO 12" PIZZAS | COMMITMENT LEVEL: DONE IN STAGES

3¾ cups all-purpose flour, plus more for rolling

¼ teaspoon active dry yeast

2 teaspoons fine sea salt

1¾ cups water

1. In a large bowl, combine the flour, yeast, and salt. Pour the water over the flour mixture and stir using a very sturdy wooden spoon. The dough won't all come together, so when the dough gets too stiff, switch to mixing with your bare hands to blend in all the flour.

2. Leave the dough in the mixing bowl. Cover it with plastic wrap and leave it to rise at room temperature until it has doubled in size. This takes about 18 hours. (If you mix the dough right after dinner, it will be ready for you when you get home from work the next day.) See "No Panic, Quick-Reference Pizza Timing Chart" for timing tips.

3. Once the dough has risen, turn it onto a well-floured surface. Divide into 4 equal pieces and shape each into a ball by tucking the edges under. Be careful not to work the dough too much. Dust the balls with flour and cover with a damp tea towel to rise for another 2 hours before stretching. If you aren't going to make the pizzas right away, seal the flour-dusted balls thoroughly in plastic wrap or slide them into a large, food-grade plastic bag. The formed dough can be refrigerated for up to 3 days.

4. An hour before you are ready to bake the pizza, place a pizza stone on a rack in the top third of the oven. Heat the oven to 550°F (or as high as your oven will go). After 45 minutes, switch the oven setting to broil.

5. Shape the dough by placing 1 ball on a floured surface and spreading it into a circle with well-floured hands. Do not use your nails, as you could tear the dough. Place your hands, knuckles facing up, beneath the dough at the 9 o'clock and 3 o'clock positions. Gently pull your hands apart, stretching but not tearing the dough. Shift each hand 1 hour clockwise and repeat the stretching.

Continue rotating and stretching the dough until you have a 10" to 12" round. If it's not 100 percent round, don't worry.

6. Place the stretched pizza dough on a peel or large wooden cutting board dusted with flour or cornmeal. Give the board a shake to ensure the dough doesn't stick. Apply toppings of choice (see pages 158 and 160 for some ideas). Be sure you don't load the pizza too heavily, or the thin crust won't be able to support the weight of the toppings.

7. Transfer the pizza to the hot stone. Place the peel at the farthest edge of the pizza stone. With a quick jerk, slide the pizza off the peel and onto the stone. Close the door quickly and set the timer for 4 minutes. I watch the dough through the oven door because it's fun to see how quickly the dough bubbles up. The crust will go from golden to burned quickly, so keep an eye on the pizza at the $3^1/_2$- to 4-minute mark. It might need an extra minute, but no pizza went longer than 6 minutes in my oven.

8. To remove the pizza, lift the nearest edge with tongs, slide the peel or board under the lifted edge, and pull the pizza onto the peel. Turn the oven to 550°F and allow the stone to heat for 10 to 15 minutes while making your next pizza. Turn the broiler back on just before the next pizza goes onto the stone.

TOPPINGS

Forget the mountains of cheese and rivers of sauce. Authentic Italian pizza crust has surprisingly little on it. A splash of sauce—if any—and a few carefully placed high-quality toppings are all you need to highlight the crust. While few people could eat an entire 12" fast-food pizza by themselves, you can (and most likely will) eat a whole thin-crust pizza unassisted. After all, it's thin and lightly garnished, so it's not a big stretch.

TIP: No pizza stone? While a baking sheet will do in a pinch, it won't cook the crust from the bottom up like a stone will. Instead, use a cast-iron griddle or cast-iron frying pan turned upside down. Just make sure you preheat it like you would the pizza stone.

NO-PANIC, QUICK-REFERENCE PIZZA TIMING CHART

24 HOURS AHEAD OF TIME: Mix the dough. Cover it and set aside at room temperature to rise.

2 HOURS AHEAD OF TIME: Form the dough into balls. Let rise at room temperature or cover and refrigerate for up to 3 days. If using refrigerated dough, let it come to room temperature before proceeding.

1 HOUR AHEAD OF TIME: Heat the oven and pizza stone.

JUST BEFORE BAKING: Stretch the dough and add toppings, being careful not to overload your pizza.

PIZZA MARGHERITA

MAKES ONE 10" TO 12" PIZZA

⅓ cup San Marzano plum tomatoes, broken into bite-size pieces

1 tablespoon chopped fresh basil

2 ounces bocconcini (3 large, cut in quarters)

2 tablespoons freshly grated Parmigiano-Reggiano cheese

1 tablespoon extra-virgin olive oil

Scatter the tomatoes, basil, and bocconcini over the dough, being sure to leave a 1" edge. Sprinkle with the Parmigiano-Reggiano. Drizzle with the oil. Bake as directed.

SAUSAGE AND ARTICHOKE PIZZA

MAKES ONE 10" TO 12" PIZZA

⅓ cup marinara sauce, commercial or homemade Either Way Marinara Sauce (page 211)

4 ounces cooked Italian sausage, sweet or hot, sliced into rounds

⅓ cup chopped marinated artichokes, drained

3 ounces shredded mozzarella (about ¾ cup)

Spread the dough with a thin layer of sauce, leaving a 1" edge. Place the sausage and artichoke over the pizza. Sprinkle with the cheese. Bake as directed.

VEGETARIAN PESTO PIZZA

MAKES ONE 10" TO 12" PIZZA

¼ cup pesto

2 tablespoons pine nuts

¼ large red bell pepper, thinly sliced

2 ounces shaved Pecorino Romano cheese (about ½ cup)

1 tablespoon extra-virgin olive oil

Spread the dough with a thin layer of pesto, leaving a 1" edge. Sprinkle with the pine nuts and bell pepper. Place the cheese on top and drizzle with the oil. Bake as directed.

CHICKEN AND HONEY PIZZA

MAKES ONE 10" TO 12" PIZZA

2 tablespoons extra-virgin olive oil

1 small clove garlic, cut into 4 pieces

¼ teaspoon dried oregano

¼ teaspoon dried marjoram

4 ounces cooked chicken breast, sliced

2 ounces chèvre cheese

2 tablespoons slivered almonds

2 tablespoons honey

Fresh cracked black pepper (optional)

Flaky sea salt

1. In a small bowl, whisk together the oil, garlic, oregano, and marjoram. Let sit for 5 to 10 minutes. At this point, the garlic pieces can be removed if you don't want a strong garlic taste.

2. Brush the dough with the herbed oil. Scatter the chicken over the pizza, leaving a 1" edge. Dot the chicken pieces with the cheese and scatter the almonds over the pizza. Drizzle with the honey and finish with a generous grinding of fresh black pepper. If there is any herbed oil left over, you can drizzle some more on as well. Bake as directed. Add a dusting of flaky sea salt before serving.

DESSERT PIZZA

MAKES TWO 10" TO 12" PIZZAS

½ cup mascarpone cheese, at room temperature

1 teaspoon grated lemon peel

2 tablespoons honey

2 tablespoons heavy cream

½ teaspoon pure vanilla extract

1 tablespoon butter

1 apple, peeled, cored, and thinly sliced

1 tablespoon packed brown sugar

¼ cup golden raisins

1 tablespoon brandy

¼ cup pine nuts

Whole nutmeg

Cinnamon stick

Flaky sea salt (such as Maldon)

1. In a small bowl, combine the cheese, lemon peel, honey, cream, and vanilla. Set aside.

2. In a medium nonstick skillet over medium heat, melt the butter. Add the apple and brown sugar. Cook, stirring, for 3 minutes, or until the apple slices are slightly soft but keep their shape. Add the raisins and brandy and cook for 1 minute, or until the raisins are plump.

3. Spread half of the reserved cheese mixture on 1 round of dough, leaving a 1" edge. Arrange half of the apple mixture evenly over the cheese mixture. Sprinkle with half of the pine nuts. If any apple-brandy sauce remains, drizzle half over the pizza. Using a microplane, grate a gentle dusting of nutmeg and cinnamon on top. Repeat with the second round of dough and remaining toppings.

4. Bake as directed. Sprinkle with flaky sea salt before serving.

ORANGE–WALNUT BLONDIES WITH MAPLE CARAMEL SAUCE

Caramel never ceases to amaze me. Technically, it's just melted sugar, but the variations seem endless. Here, slow cooking produces a soft, gentle blonde sauce so different from the bold, burnt brunette version poured over the sticky buns (page 165), it's hard to believe they're related. The blondies' brown sugar base provides a hint of butterscotch, yet another caramel variation.

MAKES 24 SQUARES | COMMITMENT LEVEL: DONE IN STAGES

1. Preheat the oven to 350°F. Grease a 13″ × 9″ baking dish.

2. *To make the blondies:* In a large bowl using an electric mixer or in the bowl of a stand mixer fitted with a paddle, beat the butter, brown sugar, and orange peel until smooth and light. Add the vanilla and orange juice and beat to combine. Beat in the eggs, one at a time.

3. In a medium bowl, combine the flour, baking powder, and salt. Stir into the butter mixture by hand or with the mixer on low. Stir in the walnuts. Pour in the baking dish and smooth with a spatula. The batter will not be deep. Bake for 25 to 30 minutes, or until a wooden pick inserted in the center comes out clean. Allow the blondies to cool in the pan on a rack.

4. *To make the sauce:* While the blondies bake (and cool), make the sauce. In a heavy saucepan, combine the cream, granulated sugar, and maple syrup. Stir over medium heat until the sugar dissolves. Increase the heat and bring the mixture to a boil. Reduce the heat to medium-low and simmer, whisking occasionally, until the sauce is caramel-colored and slightly thickened. Be patient. This process can take about 35 minutes. It's worth it.

5. Remove the sauce from the heat. Stir in the butter, orange peel, and orange liqueur. Cool the sauce slightly before using.

6. To assemble, cut the blondies into squares. Pour the slightly warm caramel sauce over individual blondies. Sprinkle with a pinch of flaky sea salt.

NOTE: Store any leftover sauce and blondies separately. The sauce will keep for several days in the refrigerator in an airtight container. The blondies will keep in an airtight container for the same length of time. Both the sauce and blondies can be frozen for up to 2 months. Once it's refrigerated, gently warm the sauce over low heat, whisking to incorporate any butter that separated out. Allow the blondies to come to room temperature before serving with the sauce and a sprinkle of flaky sea salt.

BLONDIES

1 cup unsalted butter, at room temperature

1½ cups lightly packed brown sugar

Peel of 1 orange, finely grated

1½ teaspoons pure vanilla extract

1 tablespoon orange juice

2 eggs, at room temperature

1½ cups all-purpose flour

1 teaspoon baking powder

½ teaspoon fine sea salt

1 cup toasted, coarsely chopped walnuts

MAPLE CARAMEL SAUCE

1 cup heavy cream

6 tablespoons granulated sugar

¼ cup pure maple syrup (dark is preferable)

2 tablespoons unsalted butter

Peel of 1 orange, finely grated

1 tablespoon orange-flavored liqueur

Flaky sea salt (such as Maldon)

CRANBERRY–ORANGE OATMEAL WAFFLES

I am an impatient baker. Oh, I'll tell you to get all your ducks in a row and block off enough time before starting a recipe. Sure, these are crucial steps, but I'm still impatient. So when I was craving cranberry-orange oatmeal muffins and didn't feel like waiting, I created a version in waffle form. All the flavor, half the time. It's times like these when impatience pays off.

MAKES 4 SERVINGS | COMMITMENT LEVEL: READY IN AN HOUR OR LESS

1. Heat and oil the waffle iron according to the manufacturer's instructions. Meanwhile, toast the walnuts. See the tip below for toasting ideas.

2. In a blender or food processor, combine the oats and flour. Blend or process until the oats are powdered. In a large bowl, whisk the oat mixture, baking powder, baking soda, salt, cinnamon, and brown sugar until well blended. Add the cranberries and toasted walnuts and toss to coat well with the flour mixture.

3. In a medium bowl, combine the buttermilk, orange peel, orange juice, butter, egg, and vanilla. Beat with a fork until well combined. Pour over the flour mixture and stir until combined, being careful not to overmix.

4. Cook the batter in the heated waffle iron, following the manufacturer's instructions for batter quantity and timing. Serve immediately with maple syrup, crème fraîche, or vanilla yogurt. Add a splash of Citrus and Spice Crêpe Sauce if you have any left.

NOTE: Leftover waffles can be stored in the refrigerator in an airtight container for up to a week or in the freezer for up to 2 months. To restore the waffles to their former glory (sort of), reheat by toasting them in a toaster or toaster oven or popping them back in a hot waffle iron.

TIP: When baking, I usually toast nuts in the oven. But with waffles, it seems a wasteful method. You can toast nuts on the stove top in a dry nonstick skillet over medium heat or in the microwave in 60-second bursts. Be sure to slightly undertoast them, as they will continue to cook on their own for a minute or two.

$\frac{1}{2}$ cup walnut pieces

$\frac{1}{2}$ cup quick-cooking or rolled oats

$\frac{1}{2}$ cup all-purpose flour

1 teaspoon baking powder

$\frac{1}{4}$ teaspoon baking soda

$\frac{1}{4}$ teaspoon fine sea salt

$\frac{1}{2}$ teaspoon ground cinnamon

2 tablespoons packed brown sugar

$\frac{1}{2}$ cup chopped dried cranberries

$\frac{3}{4}$ cup buttermilk

Peel of 1 navel orange, finely grated

$\frac{1}{4}$ cup fresh orange juice

2 tablespoons melted unsalted butter

1 egg, at room temperature

1 teaspoon pure vanilla extract

Maple syrup, crème fraîche (page 224), or vanilla yogurt

Citrus Sauce (page 139, optional)

BURNT CARAMEL AND SEA SALT STICKY BUNS

This is the perfect recipe for a rainy weekend. The smells of yeast and cinnamon along with the burnt caramel come together in an aroma so enticing, you'll be willing to burn your fingers to grab the first piece. Whether you have one with hot coffee, cold milk, or by itself, this tender, decadent sticky bun is best enjoyed while still warm.

MAKES ABOUT 12 | COMMITMENT LEVEL: LAZY SUNDAY AFTERNOON

1. *To make the dough:* In a measuring cup, sprinkle the yeast over the warm water. Stir the yeast into the water along with 1 teaspoon of the granulated sugar. Let stand for 5 to 10 minutes, or until foamy. Meanwhile, in a small saucepan over low heat, combine the remaining granulated sugar, butter, sour cream, milk, vanilla, and salt. Whisk until the butter has melted and the liquid is smooth. The mixture should be slightly warmer than room temperature. Add the egg and whisk to incorporate.

2. The dough can be mixed by hand in a large bowl or in the bowl of a stand mixer fitted with a dough hook. Place the yeast mixture, butter mixture, and flour in a large bowl and stir until the ingredients come together evenly. If mixing by hand, when it becomes too stiff to stir, turn the dough onto a lightly floured work surface and knead until smooth and elastic, adding more flour if the dough is sticky. If using a stand mixer, the dough is ready when it pulls away from the side of the bowl and begins to climb up the dough hook. Pull the dough from the hook and place the dough on a lightly floured work surface. Knead until smooth and elastic (about a minute). Transfer to an oiled bowl, cover with plastic wrap, and let rise for 90 minutes to 2 hours, or until doubled in size. When the dough has almost doubled, make the caramel sauce.

3. *To make the caramel sauce:* In a heavy-bottomed stainless steel saucepan with high sides, combine the granulated sugar and water. Cook over high heat, stirring occasionally, until the sugar melts and begins to boil. Keep cooking without stirring, brushing down the sides with a pastry brush dipped in water as needed. Boil 6 to 10 minutes, or until the syrup turns a deep amber color.

DOUGH

1 package (2¼ teaspoons) active dry yeast

½ cup warm water (about 100°F)

⅓ cup granulated sugar, divided

¼ cup unsalted butter

½ cup sour cream

½ cup milk

1 tablespoon pure vanilla extract

1 teaspoon fine sea salt

1 egg, at room temperature

4 cups all-purpose flour, plus more for kneading

CARAMEL SAUCE

1½ cups granulated sugar

¼ cup water

¼ cup unsalted butter

½ cup heavy cream

FILLING

¼ cup melted butter

1½ cups packed Demerara or dark brown sugar

1½ tablespoons ground cinnamon

1 cup chopped walnuts

GARNISH

Flaky sea salt (such as Maldon)

(continued on page 166)

(continued from page 165)

Be careful to keep an eye on this, as it can burn quickly. To avoid scalding yourself, put an oven mitt on the hand that will stir. Remove the pan from the heat and carefully stir in the butter. When the butter has been incorporated, stir in the cream. Remain cautious, as it might bubble up again.

4. *To assemble and add the filling:* Grease a 13″ × 9″ baking dish.

5. Punch the dough down. On a floured surface, roll the dough into a rectangle about 20″ × 12″. Drizzle the melted butter over the surface of the dough and spread to within 1″ of the edges using a pastry brush. In a small bowl, combine the Demerara or brown sugar and cinnamon. Sprinkle the buttered surface with the cinnamon sugar and walnuts. Roll up the dough, starting with the long side. Press firmly to secure the roll. Cut the dough into 12 pieces about 1½″ thick. If your ends are terribly uneven and have no filling, as is always the case with mine, trim and discard the ends.

6. Pour the caramel sauce into the baking dish. Arrange the 12 buns on top, cut side down. Cover with a tea towel and let rise for about 45 minutes, or until doubled in size.

7. While the buns rise, preheat the oven to 350°F and line a rimmed baking sheet with foil.

8. Bake for 35 to 40 minutes, or until golden brown. Remove from the oven and let stand for 5 minutes. While wearing oven mitts, place the rimmed baking sheet on top of the buns and invert them onto the baking sheet. Scrape the caramel from the baking dish over the buns. Sprinkle with flaky sea salt. Allow to cool slightly before eating.

NOTE: Sticky buns are best eaten warm but will keep in an airtight container for 2 or 3 days. Split them in half, butter the cut surfaces, and pop them under the broiler to bring them back to life. Leftovers can also be frozen for up to a month.

RHUBARB–RASPBERRY GALETTE WITH FRANGIPANE

Galettes are the ultimate in messy baking. Being free-form, the shape can be less than symmetrical, and you're not required to do any tricky lifting or fancy edging like with pies. Sometimes the filling takes "free-form" too literally and tries to wander off. If it does this during assembly, just gently herd it back in place with your hands. If it does this during baking, call it rustic. I hoard spring rhubarb for this recipe, but if you don't have any on hand, swap in blueberries, black cherries, or blackberries. Heck, why stop there? Sure, frangipane is traditionally a sweet almond paste, but try walnuts or hazelnuts instead. I won't tell. Swap lemons or limes for the orange peel.

MAKES 6 TO 8 SERVINGS | COMMITMENT LEVEL: READY IN AN HOUR OR LESS

1. Preheat the oven to 400°F.

2. *To make the pastry:* On a lightly floured board, roll the dough out to form a 12" circle. Line a large, rimmed baking sheet with parchment paper. Transfer the rolled dough to the baking sheet.

3. *To make the orange frangipane paste:* In the small bowl of a food processor or in a blender, combine the almonds, granulated sugar, egg, and vanilla. Process or blend to form a paste. Add the orange peel and pulse to blend. Spread on the pastry, leaving a 2" border all the way around.

4. *To make the fruit filling:* In a large bowl, toss the rhubarb and raspberries together. Sprinkle the vanilla and orange juice over the mixture and toss again. In a small bowl, combine the flour, granulated sugar, and tapioca. Sprinkle over the fruit and toss to coat the fruit well.

5. *To assemble:* Spoon the fruit filling evenly over the frangipane paste. Fold the pastry edge over the filling to form a rim, pleating the dough as necessary. In a small bowl, beat the egg white with a fork until fluid. Brush the top of the pastry rim with the egg white and sprinkle the crust and filling with turbinado sugar. Bake for 35 to 40 minutes, or until the crust is golden and the filling bubbles at the edges.

6. Allow the galette to cool on the baking sheet before eating. Serve as is or with vanilla ice cream, Boozy Brown Sugar Whipped Cream (page 218), crème anglaise (page 222), or crème fraîche (page 224).

NOTE: Like most pies, galettes are best eaten the day they're made, but leftovers—if there are any—can be stored in the refrigerator for up to 3 days.

PASTRY

Dough for 1 unbaked single pie crust (page 45 or your favorite recipe)

ORANGE FRANGIPANE PASTE

½ cup ground almonds

½ cup granulated sugar

1 egg

1 teaspoon pure vanilla extract

1 tablespoon finely grated orange peel

FRUIT FILLING

3 cups fresh or frozen but unthawed diced rhubarb (¼" pieces)

1 cup fresh or frozen but unthawed raspberries

1 tablespoon pure vanilla extract

1 tablespoon orange juice

¼ cup all-purpose flour

¾ cup granulated sugar

2 tablespoons minute tapioca

FINISH

1 egg white

Turbinado sugar, for sprinkling

CHOCOLATE PEAR TART WITH HONEY AND PISTACHIOS

This tart is hide-and-seek in a dessert form. Expecting a simple fruit tart, guests are often surprised— and delighted—to find a layer of dark chocolate crouching quietly beneath the golden pears and pale custard. Perhaps they thought the chocolate would arrive as a sauce. Maybe the pistachios distracted them. In our house, when this dessert arrives at the table, the first one to shout, "Ollie Ollie oxen free" gets an extra slice.

MAKES 6 TO 8 SERVINGS | COMMITMENT LEVEL: DONE IN STAGES

1 Pâte Sucrée tart shell (page 48)

4 ounces best-quality bittersweet or semisweet chocolate, finely chopped

3–4 medium dessert pears (preferably Anjou or Bartlett), ripe but still firm and unblemished

2 eggs

2 egg yolks

¾ cup sugar

Seeds of ½ vanilla bean or 1 teaspoon pure vanilla extract or 1 teaspoon vanilla paste

1½ cups heavy cream

⅓ cup honey

½ cup chopped pistachios

1. *To partially bake the crust:* Preheat the oven to 375°F. Prick the bottom of the chilled tart shell all over with a fork. Line the bottom with a piece of parchment paper or foil and fill with dried beans or pie weights. Bake for 15 to 20 minutes, or until the edges are just starting to turn golden brown and the bottom of the pastry is beginning to bake. Remove the liner and weights and bake for 10 minutes, or until lightly browned all over. Remove from the oven and allow to cool.

2. Preheat the oven to 400°F. Scatter the chocolate evenly over the bottom of the cooled tart shell. Halve and peel the pears, then core them using a melon baller to scoop out just the round seed area. Place a pear half, cut side down, on a cutting board. Slice very thin, cutting from the top of the pear almost to the bottom but keeping the pear's shape intact (so even after it's sliced, it still looks like an intact pear half). Gently press your hand down on the pear to fan the slices out. With a palate knife or spatula, transfer the fanned pear to the tart shell, with the narrow end facing the center. Repeat with the other pear halves. The tart should have a full circle of pears fanning from the center. Don't worry if there are a few gaps; any space between the pear slices will fill with custard.

3. In a small bowl, whisk the eggs, egg yolks, sugar, and vanilla. Add the cream and whisk until smooth. Pour the custard over the pears. (If you have a little custard left over, see the tip on the next page.) Drizzle the honey evenly over the pears and sprinkle with the pistachios.

4. Place the tart on a rimmed baking sheet to catch any drips. Bake in the middle of the oven for 10 minutes. Reduce the heat to 375°F and bake for 40 to 50 minutes, or until the custard has set. Allow the tart to cool completely before slicing. Serve the tart the day it's baked.

NOTE: Leftovers can be left in the tart pan, covered with plastic wrap, and stored in the refrigerator.

TIP: If you have some custard left over, make individual fruit clafoutis in ramekins. You might have enough custard for only one or two, but this provides a gluten-free alternative for guests who can't have wheat and ensures nothing gets wasted. Just grease a few ramekins, fill with 2" of sliced fruit, pour the custard over the fruit, sprinkle with granulated sugar, and bake with the pear tart for 20 minutes, or until set. Allow to cool, then serve drizzled with Chocolate Anything Sauce (page 216) and/or crème anglaise (page 222).

WHISKEY-KISSED PECAN PIE

This twist on classic bourbon-laced pecan pie is made with Canadian whiskey. My husband is a whiskey fan, and for his 50th birthday, he asked for a dessert with his favorite drink and favorite nut. This pie was the result. It's not cloyingly sweet; you can actually taste the pecans. And the booze! Toasting the pecans adds a depth of flavor that goes well with the vanilla tones in the whiskey. Whether topped with whipped cream or enjoyed as is, this pie will leave you scraping smudges of filling from your plate.

MAKES 6 TO 8 SERVINGS | COMMITMENT LEVEL: READY IN AN HOUR OR LESS

Dough for 1 deep 9" pie (page 45 or your favorite recipe)

2 generous cups pecan halves, divided

¼ cup melted salted butter

¾ cup lightly packed dark brown sugar

3 eggs, at room temperature

¾ cup amber corn syrup

1 teaspoon pure vanilla extract

3 tablespoons Canadian whiskey (such as Forty Creek)

1. Set a rack in the lower third of the oven and preheat the oven to 375°F. Line a deep 9" pie plate with the dough.

2. Roughly chop ¾ cup of the pecans. Place on a baking sheet and bake for 8 minutes, or until lightly toasted. Remove from the baking sheet and set aside to cool.

3. In a medium bowl, whisk the butter and brown sugar until the brown sugar dissolves. Add the eggs, corn syrup, vanilla, and whiskey and whisk until completely smooth. Stir in the toasted pecans. Pour the filling into the pie crust. Sprinkle the remaining 1¼ cups pecans on top of the pie.

4. Bake for 40 to 45 minutes, or until the filling is firm to the touch and the edges are golden. Allow to cool before eating. For a really tipsy experience, top with Boozy Brown Sugar Whipped Cream (page 218).

NOTE: Cover and refrigerate any leftovers. One of my testers (Don, raise your fork) swears the pie gets better with age and liked it best on day 4. No pie lasts that long in my house.

TIP: Anyone using fine single malt scotch will be slapped. If you don't have Canadian whiskey, use bourbon, rye, or dark rum. If using a blended scotch, for best results use one described as sweet, not smoky or peaty.

CHOCOLATE-ORANGE GINGERSNAP DROPS

I wanted to include a recipe for orange-ginger chocolate cheesecake. But it was too big, took too long, was too rich, had too many layers. So I took the basic trio of flavors and made a simple, decadent, truffly thing that delivered the flavors in a bite-size package. I'm calling it a drop because you simply drop the mixture into a mini paper liner. No hours of baking. No water bath. And they're so small, there's almost no guilt. These are melt-in-your-hands treats, so be sure to have napkins nearby.

MAKES ABOUT 30 | COMMITMENT LEVEL: READY IN AN HOUR OR LESS

¾ cup walnuts

1 cup roughly crushed commercial gingersnaps (about 10, or 4 ounces)

⅓ cup finely chopped crystallized ginger

Peel of 1 navel orange, finely grated

½ cup unsalted butter

¼ cup golden corn syrup or Lyle's golden syrup

7 ounces dark baking chocolate (70% cocoa), chopped into small pieces

1 egg, lightly beaten

TIP: Citrus zest can be bitter if you grate off any of the white pith. You can use the fine holes of a box grater or a microplane. Microplanes are very sharp and can take off too much zest if you're too enthusiastic. Grate with a light hand and go back and forth only two or three times before turning the orange.

1. Place 30 mini paper liners or truffle cups on a rimmed baking sheet. Set aside.

2. In a small skillet over medium heat, toast the walnuts for 5 to 8 minutes, stirring frequently to avoid burning, or until they are fragrant. Set aside and allow to cool.

3. Place the gingersnaps in a heavy resealable plastic bag and crush using a rolling pin or bottle. You will be dropping the mixture by heaping tablespoons, so you want the crumbs to be small enough to fit into the mini paper liners, but not fine like graham cracker crumbs. Empty the crumbs into a large bowl. Chop the walnuts and add to the crumbs along with the ginger and orange peel. Toss to distribute evenly and set aside.

4. In a small saucepan over medium-low heat, melt the butter and syrup. Gently bring to a boil. As soon as the sauce begins to boil, remove the pan from the heat and add the chocolate. Stir until the chocolate is fully melted and the mixture is smooth. Beat in the egg. Pour over the crumb mixture and stir until all the dry ingredients are fully coated.

5. Drop 1 heaping tablespoon of chocolate mixture into each paper liner. Cover with plastic wrap and refrigerate for several hours or overnight. Serve cold with plenty of napkins. These can get messy.

ALMOND AND FRUIT FLORENTINES

When I was a child, the woman behind the counter at the bakery would give me a free cookie. Sometimes it was a plain sugar cookie or maybe an oatmeal raisin cookie that bordered on healthy. But if the stars aligned and the fates smiled upon me, she would hand me a florentine. This was no easy-to-eat, chewy kids' cookie. This snappy treat, with its hole-laced edges, candied peel, and chocolate drizzle, was for grown-ups. I practically shook with joy when I ate one. I'm not sure if that bakery still sells florentines, but I do know I'm too old for free cookies. Neither matters now. I can make my own.

MAKES ABOUT 28 | COMMITMENT LEVEL: DONE IN STAGES

⅓ cup all-purpose flour

¾ cup sliced almonds

½ cup finely chopped dried cherries

3 tablespoons finely chopped crystallized ginger

3 tablespoons finely chopped candied orange peel

¼ cup unsalted butter

½ cup sugar

½ cup heavy cream

2 tablespoons maple syrup or honey

4 ounces semisweet chocolate, chopped into small pieces

NOTE: Florentines are best eaten the day they are made. To store, place in an airtight container with parchment paper or plastic wrap between the layers. Force yourself to consume them within 3 to 4 days lest they spoil.

TIP: Florentines are not suitable for the freezer, as freezing will spoil the texture. Guess you have to eat them right away. Shucks.

1. Place a rack in the center of the oven and preheat the oven to 350°F. (Note: I found the convection setting didn't work well with this cookie.) Line 2 baking sheets with parchment paper.

2. In a small bowl, combine the flour, almonds, cherries, ginger, and orange peel. Set aside.

3. In a saucepan over low heat, melt the butter, sugar, cream, and maple syrup or honey together. Increase the heat to medium and bring the sauce to a boil. When it begins to boil, remove the pan from the heat and stir in the reserved flour mixture, ensuring all the ingredients are evenly coated. The batter will be very runny. Let it cool for a couple of minutes to thicken slightly.

4. Using a 1-tablespoon cookie scoop, drop the batter onto the baking sheets about 3″ apart. You can fit 6 to 8 on a pan. With the back of a spoon dipped in cold water, flatten the dough so that it's very thin. Bake 1 sheet at a time for 8 to 12 minutes, or until the edges are golden brown and bubbly and the centers are light gold. Keep an eye on them until you get the timing of your particular oven.

5. Allow the cookies to cool on the baking sheet for 5 minutes before transferring to a rack, using a spatula.

6. While the cookies cool, melt the chocolate in a heatproof bowl over simmering, not boiling, water or in the microwave on medium power in 60-second bursts.

7. Place the cookies on a fresh sheet of parchment paper. Drizzle the chocolate over them. You can use a spoon, a resealable plastic bag with 1 corner snipped, or a parchment cone (see page 30 for details).

GRITTY

items with seeds, spinach, or other nuisancey bits that mess up your smile

"Do I have anything in my teeth?" My sister and I have a pact to check each other's smiles for flecks of spinach and stray poppy seeds. Not everyone is so lucky.

While fig cookies, lavash bread, and granola bars can make you smile, they can also make a mess of your grin. If you're serving these gritty dishes, set out the toothpicks, and make sure a pack of dental floss is in plain sight near the bathroom mirror. Your guests and their smiles will thank you.

GRITTY

SAVORY

SWEET

MANY-SEED LAVASH BREAD

This cracker-crisp, yeast-free Middle Eastern flatbread is almost effortless when made with a food processor. If you don't have one, mix the dough by hand with a bit of elbow grease and a sturdy wooden spoon. While it's fun to play with the kitchen equipment, people have been making variations of this bread for centuries with little more than a bowl and their hands. Enjoy these as is or with slices of cheese, a scoop of tzatziki (page 212), or a smear of aioli (page 207).

MAKES 4 LARGE OR 16 INDIVIDUAL | COMMITMENT LEVEL: DONE IN STAGES

1½ cups all-purpose flour

½ cup whole wheat flour

¾ teaspoon fine sea salt

1 tablespoon honey

¼ cup vegetable oil

½ cup water

1 tablespoon poppy seeds

1 tablespoon sesame seeds

1 tablespoon flax or chia seeds

Coarse kosher salt, for sprinkling

1. In the bowl of a food processor fitted with a steel blade, combine the flours and sea salt with a few pulses. In a small bowl, whisk together the honey, oil, and water. Pour into the flour mixture and pulse until the dough comes together. It will be stiff.

2. Turn the dough onto a lightly floured flat surface and knead a few times to form a ball. Cover and let rest at room temperature for at least 30 minutes or overnight.

3. Preheat the oven to 375°F. Line 2 baking sheets with parchment paper. In a small bowl, combine the poppy seeds, sesame seeds, and flax or chia seeds.

4. *To make individual lavash breads:* Cut the dough into 16 equal pieces and form into balls. Roll each into a length approximately 8″ long and 3″ wide. They should be about 1/16″ thick. Place on the baking sheets. Brush with water and sprinkle with the seed mixture and kosher salt. Press the topping firmly into the breads with the rolling pin or it will fall off during eating. Bake for 12 to 15 minutes, or until golden all over.

5. *To make large lavash breads:* Cut the dough into 4 equal pieces. Roll each into a rectangle about 1/16″ thick. Place on the baking sheets. Brush with water and sprinkle with the seed mixture and kosher salt. Press the topping firmly into the breads or it will fall off during eating. Bake for 16 to 18 minutes, or until golden all over.

6. Transfer to a rack to cool. Serve the individual breads as is, or break the large breads into small portions.

NOTE: Lavash bread can be stored in an airtight container for up to a week.

SPINACH AND DILL POCKETS

I find a lot of restaurant spanakopita heavy on the spinach or overly salty. These are nicely balanced with the right amount of onion and garlic. A bit of fresh (not dried) dill, mint, and lemon add lift. The only trick to these is making sure you squeeze all the water out of the spinach. Yes, this will leave you with messy tea towels, but if you don't get enough moisture out, your spanakopita will burst and leave you to perform a cleanup of another kind.

MAKES 24 | COMMITMENT LEVEL: DONE IN STAGES

1. Preheat the oven to 375°F.

2. *To make the filling:* In a sturdy colander, press the spinach to remove most of the moisture. Transfer to clean tea towels and roll, squeezing firmly to draw out the remaining moisture. This is crucial if you don't want the spinach filling to burst. (If you have strong hands and don't mind the feel of cooked spinach, you can get the moisture out by squeezing the spinach in your fist.) Place the spinach in a large bowl and set aside.

3. In a large nonstick skillet over medium heat, heat the oil. Cook the onions and garlic for 8 to 10 minutes, or until soft. Stir into the reserved spinach. Add the eggs, dill, mint, and lemon peel and blend thoroughly. Add the cheese and stir gently.

4. *To make the wraps:* Lightly dampen a tea towel. Lay the stack of phyllo sheets flat on a work surface. Cut the stack in half. You want a sheet that is approximately 9" by 12". Stack the sheets on top of each other, remove 1 sheet, and place the damp towel on top of the stack to prevent the pastry from drying out.

5. Using a pastry brush, brush the sheet lightly with oil or butter. Fold the sheet in thirds lengthwise so you have a long, thin strip 3 layers thick. Using a small cookie scoop or a spoon, place 1 tablespoon of the spinach mixture at the bottom of the sheet toward 1 side. Fold the opposite corner over the filling to form a triangle. Fold the filling up the strip, maintaining the triangle shape. Place the

FILLING

2 packages (10 ounces each) frozen chopped spinach, thawed and drained

1 tablespoon vegetable oil

2 onions, finely chopped

1 clove garlic, minced

3 eggs, lightly beaten

¼ cup minced fresh dill

2 tablespoons minced fresh mint

Peel of 1 lemon, finely grated

12 ounces feta cheese, crumbled

WRAPS

1 package (16 ounces) phyllo pastry, thawed according to package directions

½ cup vegetable oil or melted butter, for brushing

Sesame seeds or poppy seeds, for sprinkling (optional)

(continued on page 186)

(continued from page 185)

triangle seam side down on an ungreased baking sheet. Brush the top with more oil or butter, and sprinkle with sesame or poppy seeds, if using.

6. Repeat until the filling or phyllo sheets are gone. Left-over filling can be used for an omelette.

7. Bake for 12 to 15 minutes, or until golden brown. Serve immediately, as is or with tzatziki (page 212).

NOTE: Once cool, these pockets can be stored in an airtight container in the refrigerator for up to 3 days. To eat, reheat for 10 minutes in a 325°F oven. The microwave will make the phyllo soggy.

TIP: Triangles are classic for spinach, but you can roll these pockets in other shapes or even just bundle them up. See pages 49–51 for different ways to use phyllo.

ROSEMARY, APRICOT, AND PISTACHIO CRISPS

This apricot and pistachio version of Raincoast Crisps is adapted from Julie Van Rosendaal's recipe for these double-baked treats. Delightfully crisp, these crackers are bursting with dried fruit, nuts, and seeds. A hint of rosemary makes them the perfect match for cheese at parties. If for some reason they out-last the cheese, nibble them plain. Be warned, an entire batch will disappear quickly at parties, leaving the water biscuits and rice crackers feeling snubbed. Are they sweet? A little. Are they savory? A titch. Are they addictive? Totally. Bet you can't eat just one.

MAKES 6 TO 8 DOZEN | COMMITMENT LEVEL: DONE IN STAGES

1. Preheat the oven to 350°F. Coat two 8" × 4" or 9" × 5" loaf pans with cooking spray or grease liberally with butter and dust with flour.

2. In a large bowl, combine the flour, baking soda, and salt. Add the apricots, pistachios, pumpkin seeds, sesame seeds, flax seeds, and rosemary and toss to coat evenly with the flour mixture. In a small bowl, combine the buttermilk, brown sugar, and honey and stir until the sugar and honey dissolve. Add to the flour mixture and stir until just combined. Pour into the loaf pans. Bake for 35 to 45 minutes, or until golden and springy to the touch. Remove the loaves from the pans and cool on a rack. The bread is easier to slice when cool, so bake the day before or pop it in the freezer to cool it down.

3. Preheat the oven to 300°F. Using a serrated knife, slice the loaves as thinly as you can. Aim for no thicker than 1/8", if possible. Place the slices in a single layer on an ungreased baking sheet and bake for 15 minutes. Turn them over and bake for 10 minutes, or until they are crisp and deep golden brown.

2 cups all-purpose flour

2 teaspoons baking soda

1/2 teaspoon fine sea salt

1 cup chopped dried apricots

1/2 cup chopped pistachios

1/2 cup pumpkin seeds

1/4 cup sesame seeds

1/4 cup ground flax seeds

1 1/2 tablespoons chopped fresh rosemary

2 cups buttermilk

1/4 cup packed brown sugar

1/4 cup honey, warmed

TIP: These are so addictive, you might want to slice and bake one loaf and put the second loaf in the freezer (well wrapped, of course) for when the crisp craving strikes.

FIG AND APRICOT NEWTONS

The first recipe I ever created was my own version of Fig Newtons. I was 12. They were like no other cookie on the shelf. The sweet, gritty filling had too many seeds to count, and it was all wrapped in a blanket of chewy biscuit that was hard to pin down. It wasn't quite cake. It wasn't quite cookie. Unable to get the recipe just right, I would tweak the previous version each day after school—until Mom opened the cupboard to find her stash of expensive figs gone. The experiment ended due to lack of funding. Now I'm back at it with a bit of a twist, adding dried apricots and orange to make a lighter and brighter version of my childhood snack.

MAKES APPROXIMATELY 2 DOZEN | COMMITMENT LEVEL: DONE IN STAGES

1. *To make the dough:* In a large bowl using an electric mixer or in the bowl of a stand mixer fitted with a paddle, cream the butter and sugar on medium speed until light and fluffy. Beat in the egg, molasses, and vanilla.

2. In a medium bowl, whisk the flour, baking powder, and salt to combine. Using a wooden spoon or the stand mixer set on low, stir the flour mixture into the butter mixture until well combined. Turn the dough onto a large sheet of plastic wrap and refrigerate for at least 1 hour or overnight.

3. *To make the filling:* In a small saucepan over medium heat, combine the figs, apricots, sugar, honey, and orange juice. Bring to a boil. Reduce the heat and simmer for 3 to 8 minutes, or until the fruit plumps. Transfer to a blender and puree until smooth. Transfer to a small bowl. Stir in the orange peel and vanilla and set aside until cool. If you won't be baking the same day, cover and refrigerate.

4. When you're ready to assemble and bake, preheat the oven to 375°F and line 2 baking sheets with parchment paper.

5. Cut the dough in half and gently knead on a lightly floured surface to soften the dough. Once warmed, the dough will be quite soft, so handle gently. Roll 1 portion of dough into a rectangle 1/4" thick and approximately 18" long and 6" wide. Trim the edges with a knife or pizza cutter and set the trimmed dough aside. Spoon half the filling down the length of the dough, forming a 2"-wide

DOUGH

1/2 cup unsalted butter, at room temperature

3/4 cup sugar

1 egg, at room temperature

1/4 cup fancy molasses

2 teaspoons pure vanilla extract

2 cups all-purpose flour

1/2 teaspoon baking powder

1/2 teaspoon fine sea salt

FILLING

2/3 cup chopped dried figs, tough stems removed (Calimyrna or Black Mission work well)

1/2 cup chopped dried apricots

1/4 cup sugar

2 tablespoons honey

1/2 cup fresh orange juice

1 tablespoon orange peel, finely grated

1 teaspoon pure vanilla extract

(continued on page 192)

(continued from page 191)

strip down the center. Fold the edges over the filling. Cut the dough into 1$^{1}/_{2}$" bars, discarding any dough at either end that has no filling. Place on the baking sheets seam side down and bake for 12 minutes, or until the bars are slightly golden and baked all the way through. Leave on the baking sheets for a few minutes before transferring to a rack to cool.

6. While the first pan of bars bakes, roll, fill, and cut the second half of the recipe. Bake the second pan while the first is cooling.

NOTE: The bars can be stored in the refrigerator for up to 1 week. They can also be frozen for up to 2 months.

TIP: Don't waste the trimmed dough. Instead, roll it to $^{1}/_{4}$" thick, cut into 2" squares, and bake in the 375°F oven for 5 to 7 minutes, or until golden on the edges. You can eat these squares as is with a cup of tea. If you want to get fancy, smear the hot cookies with apricot jelly, sprinkle with toasted walnuts, and dust with confectioners' sugar.

CITRUS-TOPPED POPPY SEED BARS

Cookies and bars cycled through popularity in our house when I was growing up. Poppy Seed Bars were once the answer to the after-school snack attack. I loved them for their tangy lemon icing and crunchy seeds—even if they did get stuck in my braces. I'm not sure why Mom stopped making them, but I've decided to reinstate them with a bit of orange added to the mix.

MAKES 24 | COMMITMENT LEVEL: DONE IN STAGES

1. Preheat the oven to 350°F. Line a 13" × 9" baking dish with parchment paper so it overhangs on the ends for easy removal.

2. *To make the bars:* In the bowl of a stand mixer fitted with a paddle or in a large bowl using an electric mixer, beat the eggs on medium speed until well blended. Gradually beat in the brown sugar until combined. Add the oil and vanilla and beat for 1 to 2 minutes, or until light.

3. In a small bowl, whisk the flours, poppy seeds, baking powder, and salt until combined. Using a spoon or the stand mixer set on low, stir the flour mixture into the egg mixture.

4. Spread the batter into the baking dish. It will not be deep. Bake for 15 to 18 minutes, or until the edges are golden and the middle springs back when lightly touched. Leave the bars to cool in the dish. Once the bars are cool, remove them from the dish using the parchment overhang and make the icing.

5. *To make the icing:* In the bowl of a stand mixer or in a medium bowl using an electric mixer, beat the butter, orange peel, and lemon peel until pale and fluffy. Turn the speed to low and gradually blend in the confectioners' sugar, orange juice, lemon juice, and salt. Increase the speed to high and beat for 3 to 5 minutes, or until very light and fluffy. Spread the icing evenly over the cooled bars. Sprinkle with poppy seeds, if using. If you like less icing, spread it thinly and freeze the extra for next time. Let the icing set before cutting into bars.

TIP: Because of their high oil content, poppy seeds go rancid fairly quickly. To ensure you always have a usable supply on hand, store them in the freezer. They'll keep for up to a year.

BARS

2 eggs, at room temperature

1 cup packed dark brown sugar

2/3 cup vegetable oil

2 teaspoons pure vanilla extract

3/4 cup whole wheat flour

3/4 cup all-purpose flour

1/2 cup poppy seeds

1 1/2 teaspoons baking powder

3/4 teaspoon fine sea salt

ICING

1/2 cup unsalted butter, at room temperature

Peel of 1 navel orange, finely grated (about 2 tablespoons)

Peel of 1 lemon, finely grated (about 1 tablespoon)

3 cups sifted confectioners' sugar

2 tablespoons fresh orange juice

1 tablespoon fresh lemon juice

Generous pinch of fine sea salt

Poppy seeds, for garnish

NOTE: The bars can be stored in an airtight container for up to a week or frozen for up to 2 months.

BLACK AND WHITE SESAME SNAPS

With black sesame seeds added to the mix, this is a grown-up version of the candy many of us snacked on incessantly as kids. While the list of ingredients is simple, the timing is tricky. I find it best to use a candy thermometer because honey burns easily. These snaps are also very sticky, so don't give them to anyone with dentures or loose fillings—unless you're a dentist looking to drum up business.

MAKES 32 GOOD-SIZE SNAPS OR 64 SMALL | COMMITMENT LEVEL: READY IN AN HOUR OR LESS

½ cup white sesame seeds

½ cup black sesame seeds

1 cup sugar

1 cup honey

Pinch of fine sea salt

TIP: Black sesame seeds are available at Asian grocery stores. If you can't find them, just double up on the white ones. All you lose is a bit of visual drama.

1. Line a rimmed baking sheet with a silicone mat or heavy foil coated with cooking spray.

2. In a dry pan over medium heat, toast the sesame seeds until the white seeds turn light gold and are fragrant. Set aside.

3. In a heavy saucepan, combine the sugar and honey. Bring to a boil over medium heat. Cook without stirring. Occasionally, brush down the sides of the pan with a pastry brush dipped in cold water. Cook until the mixture is dark amber and a candy thermometer reaches 300°F (155°C). If you don't have a candy thermometer, drop a bit of syrup into cold water. It should form a hard, brittle thread. This takes 15 to 20 minutes.

4. Stir the reserved sesame seeds and the salt into the honey mixture. Immediately pour onto the baking sheet, spreading the mixture with a greased spatula. Wait a few minutes until the snaps begin to set. Using a greased knife, score the snaps into 32 squares. (If you want smaller snaps, score each square in half diagonally.) Let the snaps cool completely before breaking them along the score lines. Alternatively, don't score the snaps and simply break the cooled sheet to pieces and see what messy shapes appear.

NOTE: These will keep in an airtight container for up to 1 week. If it's humid, refrigerate them or they will become very sticky. Allow refrigerated snaps to come to room temperature before eating.

CHEWY FRUIT AND NUT BARS

You've seen variations of these at the high-end coffee shops. Their price tags can be as steep as the lattes'. One of the simplest recipes in this book, this is a great way to introduce children to the fun—and mess—of baking. The cereal provides crunch, the dried fruit gives a burst of flavor, and the sticky allure of melted marshmallows provides the quintessential messy factor. Best of all, the rewards are almost instantaneous. By the time the kitchen is cleaned up, the treats are cool enough to sample.

MAKES 12 TO 16 | COMMITMENT LEVEL: READY IN AN HOUR OR LESS

1. Generously butter a 13" × 9" baking dish.

2. In a very large bowl, combine the cereal flakes, cranberries, apricots, pumpkin seeds, sesame seeds, sunflower seeds, cashews, almonds, and coconut. Toss to mix well.

3. In a large saucepan over low heat or in a large microwaveable bowl using the microwave on medium power, melt the marshmallows and butter together. Stir in the salt and vanilla. Working quickly, pour over the cereal mixture and fold until all the dry ingredients are thoroughly coated. Scrape into the baking dish. Place a sheet of lightly buttered waxed paper on top of the mixture and firmly press it into the dish. Alternatively, use greased hands. Chill until firm. Cut and serve when set.

NOTE: Squares will keep in an airtight container for several days. You can also wrap individual bars in plastic wrap for lunch box treats.

TIP: You can customize these in many ways for fussy family members. Change the nuts, the dried fruit, or even the cereal. Just keep the quantities the same and don't eat any of the marshmallows along the way, and you should be just fine.

4 cups breakfast cereal flakes (cornflakes, flax flakes, or bran flakes)

$\frac{1}{4}$ cup roughly chopped dried cranberries

$\frac{1}{4}$ cup roughly chopped dried apricots

$\frac{1}{4}$ cup pumpkin seeds, raw or unsalted roasted

$\frac{1}{4}$ cup sesame seeds, raw

$\frac{1}{4}$ cup sunflower seeds, raw or unsalted roasted

$\frac{1}{4}$ cup toasted chopped cashews

$\frac{1}{4}$ cup slivered almonds

$\frac{1}{4}$ cup unsweetened coconut flakes

40 large marshmallows or 4 cups miniature marshmallows

$\frac{1}{4}$ cup unsalted butter, at room temperature

Generous pinch of fine sea salt

2 teaspoons pure vanilla extract

SOUR CHERRY AND PISTACHIO GRANOLA BARS

With dried sour cherries and crystallized ginger, this isn't the sweet candy bar version you'll find in the grocery store. While you can send these off to school with the kids, they are an unexpected and surprisingly adult appetizer when served with slices of aged Cheddar and drinks.

MAKES ABOUT 18 | COMMITMENT LEVEL: READY IN AN HOUR OR LESS

$^1/_2$ cup pistachios

$^1/_2$ cup roughly chopped dried sour cherries

$^1/_4$ cup chopped crystallized ginger

$^1/_2$ cup pumpkin seeds

$^1/_2$ cup flax or sesame seeds

1 cup ground almonds

2 cups whole rolled oats

$^1/_8$ teaspoon fine sea salt

$^1/_2$ cup unsalted butter

6 tablespoons packed dark brown sugar

$^3/_4$ cup honey or maple syrup

Peel of 1 large navel orange, finely grated

1 tablespoon pure vanilla extract

$^1/_2$ cup dark chocolate chips (optional)

1. Preheat the oven to 325°F. Line three 6-cup jumbo muffin pans with paper liners. If you don't have jumbo muffin pans, grease a 13" × 9" baking dish instead. If using chocolate chips, pop them in the freezer so they'll hold their shape better when mixed into the warm granola.

2. Sprinkle the pistachios on a rimmed baking sheet and bake for 10 minutes, or until fragrant but not browned.

3. In a large mixing bowl, combine the pistachios, cherries, ginger, pumpkin seeds, flax or sesame seeds, almonds, oats, and salt. Toss to mix well.

4. In a small saucepan over medium heat, combine the butter, brown sugar, and honey or maple syrup and bring to a boil. Reduce the heat to a simmer and cook, stirring constantly, for 5 minutes, or until the syrup thickens slightly. Keep an eye on the mixture so that it doesn't burn. Remove the pan from the heat and stir in the orange peel and vanilla. The syrup will bubble up when you add the vanilla. Stir until the syrup has calmed down.

5. Pour the hot syrup over the oat mixture. With a large spatula or wooden spoon, stir to completely cover the oats, fruits, and nuts. While the granola bar mixture is warm but not hot, add the chocolate chips, if using. Don't rush adding the chips or you will have a melty mess on your hands. Stir quickly to distribute. Using a $^1/_4$-cup ice cream scoop or spoon, scoop $^1/_4$ cup of granola into the muffin cups and press to flatten. (Alternatively, press the entire mixture into the baking dish.) Bake in the muffin pans for 15 to 18 minutes or the baking dish for 25 to 30 minutes. The bars should be golden brown on the edges and not soggy in the middle.

6. Allow the granola bars to cool in the pans. Leave muffin cup bars in the paper liners, but cut the pan version into 18 bars.

NOTE: Store in an airtight container for up to a week. You can wrap cut granola bars individually in plastic wrap and store in the refrigerator. They can also be frozen for up to 2 months.

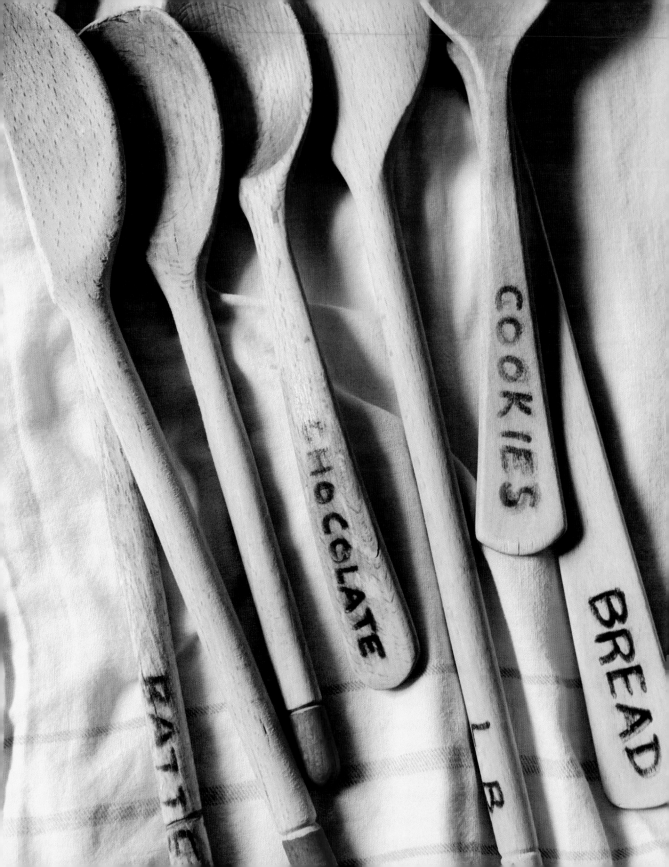

DRIPPY

sauces, dips, and toppings that splash and spill

Show me the tablecloth after dinner has been cleared and I will interpret it like a fortune-teller reading tea leaves.

If nothing but a clean, circular indentation from the plate remains, you are in control of your surroundings. You will lead a smooth, uncomplicated life.

Drips in a straight line reveal a thinker with laserlike focus. Little distracts you from your goal. You will be successful in your chosen field.

Splashes in all directions? You exhibit exuberance and unearned confidence. Blessed with more enthusiasm than knack, you will live a long, albeit messy, life.

DRIPPY

SAVORY

SWEET

EITHER WAY

LIME-CILANTRO DIPPING SAUCE

Lime, cilantro, and hot peppers are made for each other. If you're a cilantro fiend, like I am, you will want to roll in this. But don't. It's a waste of good cilantro, and the honey makes it hard to clean.

MAKES ABOUT ½ CUP | COMMITMENT LEVEL: READY IN AN HOUR OR LESS

¼ cup vegetable oil

2 tablespoons fresh lime juice (about 1 lime)

1 cup roughly chopped fresh cilantro

1 clove garlic

½ jalapeño or serrano chile pepper (optional)

1 teaspoon honey

Generous pinch of fine sea salt (or more to taste)

Fresh ground black pepper

TIP: Resist the urge to use bottled lime juice. It has additives and can impart a metallic taste to the sauce.

In a blender or the small bowl of a food processor, combine the oil, lime juice, cilantro, garlic, chile pepper (if using), honey, salt, and black pepper. Blend or process until smooth, scraping down the sides as necessary. Adjust the seasonings to taste before serving. This dipping sauce is great for Sweet Potato Samosas (page 61), Not-Too-Spicy Roasted Cauliflower (page 103), Chicken, Corn, and Cilantro Empanadas (page 124), or Smoked Paprika Corn Fritters (page 155).

NOTE: Store in an airtight container in the refrigerator for up to 5 days.

AIOLI WITH VARIATIONS

Oh sure, you can make this garlic mayonnaise by hand, but I use a blender. If anyone accuses you of cheating, hit them with a copy of Julia Childs's The Way to Cook. *Even Ms. Child didn't make mayonnaise by hand. Serve this with Rosemary and Black Olive Grissini (page 100) or anywhere you'd use mayonnaise.*

MAKES 1½ CUPS | COMMITMENT LEVEL: READY IN AN HOUR OR LESS

1. Using a microplane, mince the garlic into a blender or the small bowl of a food processor fitted with a steel blade. Add the egg yolk and pulse a few times to combine. Add the salt, lemon peel, and lemon juice and pulse again to combine. With the motor running, start adding the oil in a very, very slow stream. If you don't trust yourself to pour slowly enough by hand, drip the oil using a turkey baster. When the mayonnaise begins to thicken, add the oil a little faster without pouring it in. The mayonnaise will hold its shape but be creamier than commercial versions.

2. Taste and adjust the seasonings, adding more lemon or salt as needed and processing briefly. Spread a bit of aioli on fritters (pages 152 and 155) or use as a dip for Crispy Root Vegetable Chips (page 104).

NOTE: Use immediately or refrigerate in an airtight container for up to 5 days. The extra egg white can be used to lighten waffles or make meringues (page 68).

VARIATIONS

- Add 1 teaspoon Dijon mustard to the egg yolk and/or add 1 teaspoon grainy mustard at the end once the mayonnaise has emulsified.
- Add ¼ teaspoon smoked paprika when you add the salt.
- Substitute balsamic vinegar for the lemon juice. Stir ½ cup diced sun-dried tomatoes into the prepared aioli.

BASIC RECIPE

1 large clove garlic

1 egg yolk

½ teaspoon fine sea salt

Peel of 1 lemon, finely grated

2 teaspoons fresh lemon juice

1 cup vegetable oil or olive oil

TIP: If the mayonnaise begins to separate, don't panic. Whisk in a teaspoon of Dijon mustard with a pinch of salt. Mustard is an emulsifier and will help hold the mayonnaise together. If this doesn't work, whisk a fresh egg yolk in a clean bowl. By hand, whisk the separated mayonnaise into the fresh egg yolk a few tablespoons at a time.

FOUR TAKES ON GREMOLATA

Gremolata is really just an oil-free topping that brightens up meat and pasta. Traditionally, it's made with three simple ingredients—garlic, parsley, and lemon peel. Wanting to raise the bar, I played with the classic. Then I stumbled upon a variation with nuts, and boom—there I was making all sorts of versions and sprinkling the results on items well past the standard scope of meat and grilled foods. I know the quarter cup this recipe makes doesn't sound like much, but with gremolata, a little goes a long way.

MAKES ABOUT ¼ CUP | COMMITMENT LEVEL: READY IN AN HOUR OR LESS

BASIC RECIPE

1 clove garlic, roughly chopped

2 teaspoons finely grated citrus peel
(usually lemon)

¼ cup finely chopped herb
(usually flat-leaf parsley)

> **TIP:** Use any of these gremolatas on Spinach and Dill Pockets (page 185), fritters (pages 152 and 155), or even Chicken, Corn, and Cilantro Empanadas (page 124). Heck, sprinkle some on crêpes if you like. It's wonderfully messy if you do it by hand.

Place the garlic on a cutting board. Add the lemon peel and mince with a chef's knife, using a pivoting motion to mince the garlic and peel together. Add the herb and continue chopping until the mixture is fine.

NOTE: Without nuts, gremolata will keep for a day if covered and refrigerated. If your gremolata uses nuts, use it right away, as the nuts will get soft quickly.

VARIATIONS

- **MINT:** Substitute finely chopped mint for half the parsley.

- **ORANGE-NUT:** Substitute orange peel for the lemon and add ¼ cup finely chopped toasted hazelnuts or walnuts to the mix. (Chop the nuts separately and stir them into the herb mixture just before serving.)

- **LIME CILANTRO:** Substitute lime for the lemon and cilantro for the parsley.

EITHER WAY MARINARA SAUCE

Some people like their marinara sauce with a bit of heat. Others prefer theirs plain. By making your own, you get to choose. Either way, this sauce is delicious and versatile.

MAKES ABOUT 2½ CUPS | COMMITMENT LEVEL: READY IN AN HOUR OR LESS

1. In a large saucepan over medium-low heat, heat the oil. Cook the garlic, onion, and pepper flakes (if using), stirring occasionally, until the onion is soft. Make sure you keep the heat low enough that the garlic doesn't brown.

2. If using whole tomatoes, chop them. Add the tomatoes, along with the juice, to the onion mixture. Season with the salt and black pepper. Increase the heat to medium-high and bring the sauce to a boil. Reduce the heat and simmer, stirring occasionally, for 25 to 35 minutes, or until the sauce has thickened.

3. Remove from the heat and stir in the basil. Season to taste with additional salt and black pepper. Use immediately or cool and store in an airtight container in the refrigerator.

NOTE: The sauce will keep for up to a week in the refrigerator. It can also be frozen for up to 2 months.

2 tablespoons olive oil

4 cloves garlic, finely chopped

1 Spanish onion, finely chopped

½ teaspoon red-pepper flakes (optional)

1 can (28 ounces) tomatoes (San Marzano are the best, but regular are fine)

½ teaspoon fine sea salt (or more to taste)

Fresh ground black pepper

4–6 fresh basil leaves, slivered

TIP: San Marzano are the best canned tomatoes. If you can't find them and you are not happy with the flavor of your canned tomatoes, intensify the flavor by adding 1 to 2 tablespoons of tomato paste along with the tomatoes.

BASIC TZATZIKI WITH VARIATIONS

Most restaurant tzatziki has enough garlic to knock over a horse. I believe this yogurt spread should enhance the meal, not run over it like a steamroller. This milder, gentler version will leave you more socially acceptable and give the other menu items a fighting chance.

MAKES ABOUT 1½ CUPS | COMMITMENT LEVEL: DONE IN STAGES

1 cup Greek yogurt

1 or 2 cloves garlic

1 piece (6") English cucumber

½ teaspoon fine sea salt

Fresh ground black pepper

TIP: If you can't find Greek yogurt, you can make your own with standard plain yogurt. Place a strainer lined with two or three basket-shaped coffee filters or several layers of cheesecloth over a bowl. Empty a tub of plain yogurt into it, cover with plastic wrap, and set in the refrigerator for several hours or even overnight to drain. The yogurt will be reduced by at least half. Discard the yogurt water and use the strained yogurt in tzatziki.

1. Place the yogurt in a medium bowl. Using a microplane, grate the garlic into the yogurt. Stir to mix well.

2. Using the large holes of a box grater, grate the cucumber. Place the cucumber in a strainer over the sink and gently press out the excess water with the back of a ladle or your hand. Stir the drained cucumber into the yogurt. Add the salt and pepper, mix well, and adjust spices to taste, if necessary. Cover and refrigerate for at least a couple of hours to let the flavors blend. I think it's best the next day.

NOTE: The tzatziki will keep for up to 5 days in the refrigerator in an airtight container.

VARIATIONS

- Use roasted garlic instead of raw for a delicate garlic taste.
- Add ¼ cup minced fresh dill.
- Add 2 tablespoons minced fresh dill and 1 tablespoon minced fresh mint.
- Add the peel of half a lemon (with or without dill and/or mint).
- Add ⅓ cup finely chopped cilantro. This is good served with Indian food such as samosas (page 61).

BALSAMIC ROASTED STRAWBERRIES

Delightfully gloppy, these roasted berries will spill all over the pan—and your ice cream, yogurt, or scones. Be sure to use a good-quality balsamic on them. If you can drink a sip straight from a spoon, it will be fine. If the vinegar makes you pucker, save it for salad dressings and splurge on a small jar of quality balsamic.

MAKES A PITIFULLY SMALL AMOUNT FOR 2 | COMMITMENT LEVEL: READY IN AN HOUR OR LESS

1. Preheat the oven to 425°F. Line a rimmed baking sheet with parchment paper.

2. In a medium bowl, toss the strawberries with the vinegar. Spread on the baking sheet, making sure they are in a single layer and not piled on top of each other. Sprinkle with the brown sugar.

3. Bake for 10 to 15 minutes, or until the sugar bubbles and the berries are tender. Allow to cool for a few minutes before transferring the berries and juice to a bowl. Serve on top of Ginger and Vanilla Scones (page 87) with or without crème fraîche (page 224), spoon them over ice cream, or use instead of fresh berries for Ginger-Crusted Strawberry Mascarpone Tart (page 127).

NOTE: If not using immediately, the berries can be covered and refrigerated for up to 3 days. Yeah, like that's gonna happen.

2 cups hulled and halved fresh ripe strawberries (halve small berries, quarter big ones)

1 tablespoon good-quality balsamic vinegar

2 tablespoons packed brown sugar

TIP: Size matters when it comes to berries, but in this case, bigger isn't necessarily better. Small berries from local growers will deliver more flavor and have a better texture than their gigantic imported counterparts.

CHOCOLATE ANYTHING SAUCE

Everyone in my family loves chocolate, but no one can agree on which flavor lends itself best as its partner. Select the liqueur depending on your preferences or what you plan to drizzle it over.

MAKES ABOUT 1 CUP | COMMITMENT LEVEL: READY IN AN HOUR OR LESS

½ cup heavy cream

4 ounces good-quality semisweet chocolate, roughly chopped

Pinch of fine sea salt

2 tablespoons liqueur (such as orange, raspberry, mint, ginger, peach schnapps, cherry, or coffee)

TIP: This sauce isn't overly sweet, since it's designed to go on sweet things. If you want a sweeter sauce, use 2 ounces of semisweet chocolate and 2 ounces of sweet chocolate.

1. In a small, heavy saucepan over medium-low heat, bring the cream to a simmer. When steam begins to rise on the surface and bubbles form around the edge, remove the pan from the heat. Add the chocolate and salt. Let the chocolate sit a minute until it begins to melt, then gently stir until it has dissolved and the sauce is smooth.

2. Stir in the liqueur of your choice. Serve while still warm on ice cream, crêpes, waffles, or profiteroles (page 135).

NOTE: Once cooled, the sauce can be refrigerated for up to a week. To rewarm, gently heat in a heatproof bowl over simmering water or in the microwave on low power.

BOOZY BROWN SUGAR WHIPPED CREAM

I was out of white sugar but needed some whipped cream, so I tried brown sugar. For some reason (I'm looking at you, husband dear), there was a bottle of whiskey on the counter. One thing led to another, and a tipsy, caramel-kissed cream was the result. A pinch of salt softens the edges.

MAKES ABOUT 1½ CUPS | COMMITMENT LEVEL: READY IN AN HOUR OR LESS

2 tablespoons firmly packed dark brown sugar

1–2 tablespoons whiskey, bourbon, rye, or rum (use less for a lighter whipped cream)

½ teaspoon pure vanilla extract

1 cup heavy cream, very cold

⅛ teaspoon fine sea salt

In the bowl of a stand mixer fitted with a whisk or in a medium bowl using an electric mixer, stir the sugar, liquor, and vanilla until the sugar is dissolved. Pour in the cream and salt. Beat on low speed for a few seconds to blend. Increase the speed to high and beat until stiff peaks form.

NOTE: Use immediately or cover and refrigerate until you're ready to use it later that day.

TIP: What do you do with boozy whipped cream? Lick the beaters and some ideas will come. Add orange liqueur and serve it with Citrus and Spice Crêpes (page 139), whiskey with Whiskey-Kissed Pecan Pie (page 172), or raspberry liqueur with Rhubarb-Raspberry Galette (page 169). It makes a surprising filling for profiteroles (page 135) and can boost the tipsy factor in Boozy Chocolate Torte (page 131). One tester made it with Kahlúa and put it in her coffee. As long as there are no children present, use it anywhere you would dollop sweetened whipped cream.

SALTED CARAMEL SAUCE

Caramel sauce requires all your senses. You need to see the sugar, smell it as it bubbles away, and have your muscles at the ready to dodge the spatters. This sauce takes the caramel to the brink of burning, so use a stainless steel or enamel-coated pot. Nonstick will mask the color, and you can slip from perfect to burned in seconds.

MAKES ABOUT 1½ CUPS | COMMITMENT LEVEL: READY IN AN HOUR OR LESS

2 cups sugar

¼ cup water

½ cup unsalted butter, cubed

1 cup heavy cream

½ teaspoon flaky sea salt (such as Maldon)

TIP: If despite your best efforts you get sugar crystals in your finished sauce, simply strain the sauce through a fine mesh strainer.

1. In a heavy saucepan over medium heat, combine the sugar and water. Heat, stirring gently, until the sugar starts to melt and begins to boil. When it does, stop stirring but continue to cook the sugar, swirling the pan occasionally to ensure the sugar melts evenly. If the sugar begins to crystallize on the side of the pan, brush down the sides with a pastry brush dipped in cold water. The caramel is ready when it turns dark amber and gentle whiffs of steam (not smoke) rise from the surface. If you have a candy thermometer, 350°F is the key. Watch carefully because the sauce will burn quickly. The second it reaches this stage, remove the pan from the heat.

2. Grab a whisk and an oven mitt to prevent your stirring hand from getting scalded by steam. Add the butter. Be careful—the mixture will spatter. Whisk in the butter. When it has dissolved, carefully whisk in the cream. Don't relax just yet. The mixture will spatter with this addition, too. Whisk in the salt.

3. Allow the caramel sauce to cool slightly. Use on profiteroles (page 135), pour over ice cream, salvage day-old sticky buns (page 165), or use as a dip for apples. Yeah, apples. That'll make this healthy.

NOTE: Store unused sauce in an airtight container. It will keep in the refrigerator for up to 2 weeks.

NUTMEG BRANDY SAUCE

This is an old-fashioned kind of sauce. Simple, straightforward, not a lot of steps. But don't let the simplicity fool you. You might find yourself tasting and tasting and tasting again just to be sure you've got it right.

MAKES ABOUT 1½ CUPS | COMMITMENT LEVEL: READY IN AN HOUR OR LESS

1. In a medium saucepan over medium heat, combine the butter, brown sugar, brandy, nutmeg, and salt. Stirring gently with a wooden spoon, heat the sauce until it becomes liquid. Bring to a simmer and cook for 2 minutes for a thin sauce, 5 minutes for a slightly thicker sauce.

2. Remove from the heat, allow to cool slightly, and whisk. Serve warm over profiteroles (page 135), crêpes, or ice cream. It also goes well on cake that has dried out a bit.

NOTE: The cooled sauce can be refrigerated in an airtight container for up to a week or frozen for later use for up to 2 months.

1 cup unsalted butter

¾ cup lightly packed dark brown sugar

5 tablespoons brandy

⅛ teaspoon freshly grated nutmeg

¼ teaspoon fine sea salt

TIP: Avoid preground nutmeg. What it gains in convenience it loses in flavor. Instead, buy whole nutmeg and grate it on a microplane. If you have a container of ground nutmeg in the cupboard and want to use it up (replacing it with whole nutmeg, of course), you might have to bump the amount to ¼ teaspoon.

CRÈME ANGLAISE

This is a classic dessert sauce that never goes out of style. It can be served warm or cold on almost any dessert, especially those with fruit. It even saved Thanksgiving for one recipe tester who forgot to sweeten her pumpkin pie. Instead of tossing it, she served it covered in crème anglaise. No one complained. Some even asked for seconds.

MAKES ABOUT 1½ CUPS | COMMITMENT LEVEL: DONE IN STAGES

½ cup heavy cream

½ cup whole or 2% milk

½ vanilla bean

4 egg yolks

¼ cup sugar

TIP: Don't have a vanilla bean? For this recipe, use 1½ teaspoons vanilla paste (which has the seeds) or 1½ teaspoons pure vanilla extract.

1. In a small saucepan over medium heat, combine the cream, milk, and vanilla bean and heat until bubbles form around the edge of the pan. Remove the pan from the heat, cover, and let steep for 20 to 30 minutes to allow the vanilla bean to infuse the cream mixture.

2. Remove the vanilla bean, split it lengthwise with a sharp knife, and scrape the seeds into the cream mixture. (Don't throw out the pod. It can be used to make vanilla sugar. See page 39.)

3. In a medium bowl, whisk the egg yolks with the sugar. Whisk a ladle of the warm cream mixture into the yolks to warm them. Add the rest of the cream in a thin, steady stream, whisking the entire time. Return the mixture to the saucepan. Stirring constantly, cook over medium heat for 2 to 3 minutes, or until the sauce is thick enough to coat the back of a spoon.

4. Place a fine mesh strainer over a clean bowl and strain the sauce. If serving warm, allow to cool slightly. If serving cold, place plastic wrap directly on the sauce's surface and refrigerate for at least 1 hour, or until chilled. Drizzle on Rhubarb-Raspberry Galette (page 169), Extra-Crispy Peach and Blueberry Crisp (page 130), Citrus and Spice Crêpes (page 139), or any dessert that takes your fancy.

NOTE: Unused sauce can be stored in the refrigerator in an airtight container for up to 3 days.

BERRY SAUCE

As a kid, I was jealous of friends who got to pour blueberry-flavored sauce from the grocery store over their pancakes. All Mom would give us was pure maple syrup. Oh, the injustice. Today? The tables have turned. But I still like berry sauce—only homemade. Unlike commercial syrups that are overly sweet, this sauce is more berry than sugar. Growing up has its advantages.

MAKES 1 TO 1½ CUPS | COMMITMENT LEVEL: READY IN AN HOUR OR LESS

1. In a medium saucepan over medium heat, gently combine the berries, water, syrup, and vanilla and bring to a boil. Reduce the heat and simmer, stirring occasionally, for 3 to 5 minutes, or until the berries are tender. The timing varies with the berries you have used.

2. Using an immersion blender, food processor, or regular blender, puree the mixture. Place a fine mesh strainer over a clean bowl and press the puree through using the back of a ladle to remove the seeds and skin. Taste, adding more syrup as necessary. Use while still slightly warm over ice cream, waffles (page 163), or crêpes (page 139). Raspberry sauce goes great over Raspberry-Stuffed French Toast (page 141), and the blueberry version can enliven the Blueberry-Lime Cornmeal Muffins (page 85) as they reach the end of their shelf life.

NOTE: Leftover sauce will keep for up to a week if refrigerated in an airtight container. It can also be frozen for up to 2 months.

2 cups fresh or frozen and unthawed berries (blueberries, raspberries, and blackberries work best, either on their own or mixed)

1 tablespoon water

¼ cup golden syrup or amber corn syrup

½ teaspoon pure vanilla extract

HOMEMADE CRÈME FRAÎCHE

Chefs love this thick, slightly tangy cream. Playing nicely with both sweet and savory dishes, it complements fresh fruit, crowns cobblers, and garnishes soups. Because it won't curdle when boiled, it's ideal for finishing hot dishes like beef stroganoff. While it might be readily available in France, it's almost impossible to find in grocery stores. Should you be lucky enough to come across some in a specialty shop, its price will be as high as its fat content. Fortunately, you can make it at home for about the cost of heavy cream. No special equipment required.

MAKES 1 TO 1½ CUPS | COMMITMENT LEVEL: DONE IN STAGES

1 cup heavy cream

2 tablespoons buttermilk, ½ cup sour cream, or ½ cup Balkan yogurt

1. In a small bowl, combine the cream and buttermilk, sour cream, or yogurt. Cover with plastic wrap and set on the counter. Leave at room temperature for 8 to 24 hours. (Don't panic. It will not go bad. You need to leave the cream at room temperature so the bacteria in the dairy will thicken the cream. Think yogurt, only with 75 times the butterfat.)

2. Stir. Cover with fresh plastic wrap and refrigerate. Use on Rhubarb-Raspberry Galette (page 169), in soups, and on waffles (page 163) or crêpes (page 139), or drizzle over Extra-Crispy Peach and Blueberry Crisp (page 130).

NOTE: Once refrigerated, crème fraîche will keep for up to 10 days. Yeah. Right.

ACKNOWLEDGMENTS

If cookbooks were movies, the closing credits would rival those of Peter Jackson's *Lord of the Rings*. So many hands helped at every stage—from conception to the final book. I owe each of you more gratitude than there are grains of sugar in my pantry. Let's have a big, butter-smeared round of applause for the following people who worked behind the scenes:

My mother, father, sisters, brothers-in-law, niece, and numerous friends who tasted recipes and provided feedback without letting me get away with "good enough." Thanks for falling on that sword.

Lisa O'Connell, for suggesting I write down my thoughts about food, which started this whole pastry ball rolling. You lost a playwright, but you gained a grateful friend. And a lifetime supply of cookies.

My intrepid agent, Brandi Bowles. You saw I had what I didn't believe I possessed—a book deep inside me. Without you, I'd be pie filling without the crust.

Monica Bhide, for your insight and encouragement when I wasn't sure. You were. And that made all the difference.

Kirsten Hanson, for being the first editor to sign me on. Your calm advice, guidance, and warm personality kept the manuscript on track. Thanks for encouraging me to embrace exuberance and for understanding the need to fingerpaint in your best party dress.

Elissa Altman, for making this book far better than I ever imagined possible. Your thoughtful edits and careful observations made me a better, more joyous writer.

Amy King and the Rodale design team, for making the layout worthy of Elissa's rock-star editorial skills.

Ryan Szulc, for your artistry, skill, unfailing good humor, consummate professionalism, and Zen working atmosphere despite shooting during a record-breaking heat wave. Your photography brought me to happy tears more than once. To Madeleine Johari, for bringing your perfect, well-researched props and gorgeous model hands. Noah Witenoff, for your eye-catching food styling and ability to make me laugh even when the humidity was melting the food. Jill Snider, for baking, baking, baking and making it look just as I intended. Matt Gibson, for your irrepressible cheerfulness and nonstop offers of caffeine. I can't imagine working with a better team.

My recipe testers, who opened your kitchens, cranked up your ovens, and provided solid, helpful, bar-raising feedback on every recipe. Chocolate-smeared kisses go out to: Cheryl Arkison, Kathryn Bennett, Monica Bhide, Anita Bridge, Jacqui Cohen, Lori Desormeaux, Sarah Fischer, Barb Freda, Wendy Gacparski, Karen Gelbart, Jay Godfrey, Judith Godfrey, Lisa Waterman Gray, Dan Kelley, Theresa Kolisnyk, Myriam Léger, Don Lesser, Kathe Lieber, Linda Lucero, Lisa MacColl, Jennifer Mackenzie, Sandra McHugh, Caroline Mitchell, Lisa O'Connell, Anja Sonnenberg, Debbie Spadafore, Linda Tambunan, Stephanie Tjelios, Marijke Vroomen-Durning, and Lana Watkins.

Julie Van Rosendaal, for sharing your addictive recipe for Raincoast Crisps without hesitation. Your generosity and friendship are an inspiration. Calgary is lucky to have you.

My husband, Andrew, who for 6 months lived on test recipes with only the occasional steak and glass of scotch as relief. You never complained. You only encouraged. And every day proved I was smart to have married you.

GLOSSARY

BEAT: To use a circular motion to change the texture of ingredients. Beating softens butter, incorporates air, smooths a lumpy batter, or mixes wet and dry ingredients together. It can be done with a whisk, a spoon, an electric mixer, or a stand mixer.

BOIL: To heat a liquid so that big bubbles vigorously break the surface. At sea level this occurs at 212°F (100°C).

CARAMELIZE: To melt sugar until it turns amber or dark brown. This process changes the flavor of the sugar as well as the color. The term applies to both plain sugar (as in caramel sauce, page 220); as well as the sugar that naturally occurs in food (as in caramelized onions, page 76).

CHILL: To refrigerate something until it's cold all the way through.

CURDLE: When a milk product separates and forms grainy clumps. Milk, yogurt, and sour cream can curdle when overcooked or an acid is added to it. Cream is the one dairy product that won't curdle from heat or acid.

DRAIN: To remove unwanted liquids from food. Often done using a mesh strainer or colander.

DRIZZLE: To pour a liquid such as honey, melted chocolate, sauce, or oil over food in a very fine stream using a back-and-forth motion.

DUST: To put a fine coating of sugar, cocoa powder, or flour on the surface of something. The best way to dust is to put the ingredient in a fine mesh strainer and tap it lightly over the surface. Alternatively, you can sprinkle with your hands.

FOLD: To combine ingredients gently by sliding a spoon or spatula across the bottom of the bowl, up the side, and turning the mixture over. This is done to keep air in the batter and is used most often with whipped egg whites or whipped cream. The heavier mixture is usually added to the lighter.

KNEAD: A fold-and-press motion performed to develop the glutens in flour. Used most often with yeasted dough, kneading can be done by hand or with a stand mixer fitted with a dough hook.

MELT: To turn a solid into a liquid by heating it.

NONREACTIVE: A nonreactive pot, pan, or bowl is one that doesn't react chemically with food. Some recipes specify nonreactive vessels when an acid—like lemon juice or tomato sauce—can leave a metallic taste in the finished dish. Nonreactive materials include stainless steel, enamel, glass, clay, and even plastic. When a recipe calls for a nonreactive pan, do not use copper, aluminum, or untreated cast iron.

PEEL: The thin outer layer of citrus fruit (also known as zest) or the act of removing it. You can grate citrus using a box grater or microplane or remove it in long, thin strips using a zester.

PREHEAT: To heat a cooking device before baking or cooking. The term usually applies to ovens, but you can also preheat griddles and broilers.

PUREE: To make something smooth by grinding it with the blade of a food processor or blender.

REDUCE: To boil off some of the liquid in a sauce in order to concentrate the flavor and make the sauce thicker.

SCORE: To make a shallow cut in the surface of pastry or yeast breads. It can be used to create a design (such as in the tarts on pages 127 and 138) or to make final cuts easier (as with the sesame snaps on page 196).

SEIZE: When melted chocolate turns grainy and lumpy because it came in contact with moisture.

SIFT: To remove lumps from a powder—most often flour, cocoa powder, or confectioners' sugar. This is usually done using a mesh strainer.

SIMMER: To heat a liquid to just below the boiling point so that small bubbles will gently break the surface.

STRAIN: To remove the liquid from an ingredient by letting it drain through a sieve.

TOSS: To mix ingredients together by lightly lifting and releasing them. Do this when you wish to combine ingredients but maintain their shape. For example, you don't want to break the raspberries when coating them with flour in Rhubarb-Raspberry Galette (page 169).

WHIP: To rapidly beat a liquid (usually egg whites or heavy cream) until it becomes full of air and can form peaks. This can be done using a whisk, an electric mixer, or a stand mixer.

WHISK: To use a whisk to blend ingredients together.

COMMON MEASUREMENTS AND EQUIVALENTS

TEASPOONS, TABLESPOONS, AND CUPS

1 tablespoon = 3 teaspoons

4 tablespoons = $\frac{1}{4}$ cup

BUTTER

By the pound, stick, or ounce, here's how butter measures up.

STICK	CUPS	TABLESPOONS	OUNCES *(BY WEIGHT)*
4 sticks	2 cups	32 tablespoons	16 ounces
3 sticks	1$\frac{1}{2}$ cups	24 tablespoons	12 ounces
2 sticks	1 cup	16 tablespoons	8 ounces
1$\frac{1}{2}$ sticks	$\frac{3}{4}$ cup	12 tablespoons	6 ounces
1$\frac{1}{3}$ stick	$\frac{2}{3}$ cup	10 tablespoons + 2 teaspoons	5.5 ounces
1 stick	$\frac{1}{2}$ cup	8 tablespoons	4 ounces
$\frac{2}{3}$ stick	$\frac{1}{3}$ cup	5 tablespoons + 1 teaspoon	2.75 ounces
$\frac{1}{2}$ stick	$\frac{1}{4}$ cup	4 tablespoons	2 ounces
$\frac{1}{4}$ stick	$\frac{1}{8}$ cup	2 tablespoons	1 ounce
$\frac{1}{8}$ stick	—	1 tablespoon	0.5 ounce

CITRUS FRUIT

While you can never truly compare apples to oranges, sometimes you can't compare oranges to oranges, either. As a general guideline, here's what most recipes expect from citrus fruit.

FRUIT	JUICE	PEEL
1 navel orange	½ cup	2 tablespoons
1 lemon	3 tablespoons	1 tablespoon
1 lime	2 tablespoons	2 teaspoons

CHEESE

How much cheese do you need? Whether the recipe uses weight or volume, most cheeses fall into this scale.

OUNCE	SHREDDED
8 ounces (½ pound)	2 cups
4 ounces	1 cup
2 ounces	½ cup
1 ounce	¼ cup

OVEN TEMPERATURES

FAHRENHEIT (°F)	CELSIUS (°C)	FAHRENHEIT (°F)	CELSIUS (°C)
225	110	400	200
250	120	425	220
275	135	450	230
300	150	475	245
325	160	500	260
350	175	525	275
375	190	550	285

ADJUSTING CAKE PAN SIZE

Pan acquisition is a dangerous addiction that can result in a maimed credit rating. However, ignoring recipe requirements is not the solution. A head-in-the-flour-bin approach can lead to culinary disaster, just as buying every pan on the market can lead to financial ruin.

Using the right-size pan is important, but it doesn't mean you need more pans. It just means you need to know how to fudge it. This chart will get you out of most pan-induced panics.

PANS THAT HOLD 8 CUPS BATTER	PANS THAT HOLD 10 CUPS BATTER
8" × 8" square	9"× 9" square
9" round	10" round
11"× 7" rectangle	13"× 9" rectangle

Need more?

If math gives you a rash, photocopy the chart above, paste it where you can refer to it often, and don't deviate from the chart. For those who like a challenge, here is how to calculate how to bake a cake intended for a 9″ round pan, using an 8″ round pan. The key is to measure the surface area.

1. CALCULATE THE SURFACE AREA OF BOTH PANS. The formula for round pans is pi ($\pi = 3.14$) × the radius squared.

- *Surface area for 9″ round pan = 3.14 × 4.5 × 4.5 = 63.58*
- *Surface area for 8″ round pan = 3.14 × 4 × 4 = 50.24*

2. CALCULATE THE PERCENTAGE OF THE SMALLER PAN. Here's how much surface area the 8" round pan offers versus the 9" pan.

- *(50.24 ÷ 63.58) × 100 = 79%*

That's 80 percent in my world. In order for the recipe to work, the 8″ round pan should hold only 80 percent of the batter intended for its 9″ counterpart. So pour 80 percent of your batter into the 8″ pan. (Use a scale to do this.) This ensures the height of the batter is approximately the same as the original recipe intended and your cake won't spill over.

And just what do you do with the remaining 20 percent? Bake cupcakes.

BUT WAIT. THERE'S MORE!

This is where math ends and the alchemy begins. You have to reduce the baking time "slightly." How much is "slightly"? That depends on too many factors to calculate accurately. Start by reducing the baking time by 5 to 10 minutes, check the cake, and estimate additional baking time from there—if needed.

EMERGENCY SUBSTITUTIONS

It happens. Someone who shall remain nameless eats the last of the eggs or puts the milk back in the fridge with only a drop left. Yogurt goes bad, or that jar of corn syrup turns out to be barbecue sauce. Sometimes you have to make substitutions.

You'll notice the heading above says "Emergency." The recipes in this book were developed with a specific outcome in mind. While they're reasonably flexible, substitutions can change the taste, color, and/or texture of the final dish.

But an altered baked good is better than none. So here we go . . .

FLOUR

IF YOU DON'T HAVE	SUBSTITUTE
1 cup all-purpose flour	• 1 cup + 2 tablespoons cake, pastry, or cake and pastry flour (for pastry or light baked goods) • 1 cup bread flour (for heavy baked goods)
1 cup bread flour	• 1 cup all-purpose flour • 1 cup whole wheat flour (structure won't be as strong)
1 cup sifted cake, pastry, or cake and pastry flour	• 1 cup – 2 tablespoons all-purpose flour + 2 tablespoons cornstarch added in its place
1 cup whole wheat flour	• 1 cup – 3 tablespoons all-purpose flour + 3 tablespoons wheat germ added in its place
1 cup panko crumbs	• 1 cup crushed melba toasts • 1 cup crushed saltines • 1 cup bread crumbs

SUGAR AND SWEETENERS

IF YOU DON'T HAVE	SUBSTITUTE
1 cup granulated sugar	• 1 cup packed light brown sugar (baked goods will be moister and chewier) • 1 cup superfine sugar • 1¾ cups confectioners' sugar (baked goods will be less crisp) • 1 cup turbinado sugar (might have to work to dissolve sugar)
1 cup light brown sugar	• 1 cup granulated sugar + 2 tablespoons molasses • ½ cup dark brown sugar + ½ cup granulated sugar • 1 cup Demerara sugar
1 cup dark brown sugar	• 1 cup Demerara sugar • 1 cup light brown sugar + 1 tablespoon molasses • 1 cup granulated sugar + 3 tablespoons molasses
1 cup confectioners' sugar	• ½ cup granulated sugar + ¾ teaspoon cornstarch, finely ground together
1 cup corn syrup	1 cup granulated sugar + ¼ cup water
1 cup honey	• 1¼ cups granulated sugar + ¼ cup liquid • ½ cup granulated sugar + ¾ cup maple syrup or corn syrup
1 cup golden syrup	• 1 cup amber corn syrup

RISING AGENTS

IF YOU DON'T HAVE	SUBSTITUTE
8-gram package (2¼ teaspoons) active dry yeast	• 2¼ teaspoons instant yeast (add to dry ingredients and cut rising time in half)
8-gram package (2¼ teaspoons) instant dry yeast	• Equal amount of bread yeast added to dry ingredients • Equal amount of active dry yeast, but sprinkled over warm water and left for 5 to 10 minutes until it foams, then added to wet ingredients
1 teaspoon baking powder	¼ teaspoon baking soda + ½ teaspoon cream of tartar + ¼ teaspoon cornstarch
1 teaspoon baking soda	Sorry. You're out of luck. The only substitution I could find was for equal parts potash. Not in my kitchen.

EGGS

IF YOU DON'T HAVE	SUBSTITUTE
1 large egg	• 2 yolks + 1 tablespoon cold water (will be richer) • 3 tablespoons mayonnaise (for cakes) • 3 tablespoons ground flax + $\frac{1}{8}$ teaspoon baking powder + 3 tablespoons water (muffins and quick breads) • $\frac{1}{2}$ teaspoon more baking powder + $\frac{1}{4}$ cup extra liquid (for muffins)
1 teaspoon cream of tartar (for whipping egg whites)	• 1 teaspoon white vinegar or lemon juice

DAIRY

IF YOU DON'T HAVE	SUBSTITUTE
1 cup buttermilk	• 1 tablespoon lemon juice or white vinegar, topped with enough milk to make 1 cup (let stand for 5 to 10 minutes) • $\frac{1}{2}$ cup plain yogurt + $\frac{1}{2}$ cup milk • Buttermilk made from buttermilk powder (follow package directions—for baking only)
1 cup 2% milk	• 1 cup whole milk (results will be richer) • 1 cup 1% milk (baked goods will be drier and fall apart more easily) • $\frac{1}{2}$ cup evaporated milk + $\frac{1}{2}$ cup water • 2 tablespoons melted butter + enough fat-free milk to make 1 cup
Sour cream	• 1 cup Balkan or Greek yogurt (for garnish)
Crème fraîche	• $\frac{1}{2}$ cup sour cream + $\frac{1}{2}$ cup cream
1 cup mascarpone	• $\frac{1}{2}$ cup cream cheese + $\frac{1}{2}$ cup sour cream (blended) • $\frac{3}{4}$ cup cream cheese + $\frac{1}{4}$ cup heavy cream (blended)

BUTTER AND FATS

IF YOU DON'T HAVE	SUBSTITUTE
1 cup unsalted butter	• 1 cup salted butter *minus* ¼ to ½ teaspoon salt from recipe • 1 cup margarine (less flavor, and baking will be less crisp) • 1 cup shortening (cookies will be crisper but less flavorful) • 1 cup shortening or lard (for pastry, but moisture will need to be adjusted)
1 cup vegetable oil	1 cup grapeseed, light olive, soybean, canola, peanut, safflower, or sunflower oil

CHOCOLATE

IF YOU DON'T HAVE	SUBSTITUTE
1 ounce unsweetened chocolate	• 3 tablespoons natural cocoa powder + 1 tablespoon butter, vegetable oil, or shortening
1 ounce bittersweet or semisweet chocolate	• ½ ounce unsweetened chocolate + 1 tablespoon sugar • 3 tablespoons cocoa powder + 1 tablespoon sugar + 1½ teaspoons butter, vegetable oil, or shortening
3 tablespoons natural cocoa powder	• 3 tablespoons Dutch-processed cocoa powder, and omit the baking soda
3 tablespoons Dutch-processed cocoa powder	• 3 tablespoons natural cocoa powder plus a pinch of baking soda
1 cup semisweet chocolate chips	• 1 cup milk or white chocolate chips • 1 cup chopped nuts (walnuts and pecans are the most common)

HERBS AND SPICES

IF YOU DON'T HAVE	SUBSTITUTE
1 tablespoon fresh herbs (such as rosemary, thyme, oregano)	1 teaspoon dried herbs
1 teaspoon mace	• 1 teaspoon nutmeg • 1 teaspoon allspice • 1 teaspoon apple pie spice
1 teaspoon pure vanilla extract	• $\frac{1}{3}$ vanilla bean pod, split and scraped (added at beginning of cooking process) • 1 teaspoon vanilla bean paste
1 vanilla bean	• 1 tablespoon vanilla extract (added toward end of cooking) • 1 tablespoon vanilla bean paste

NUTS, SEEDS, AND DRIED FRUIT

IF YOU DON'T HAVE	SUBSTITUTE
1 cups nuts (any kind)	• 1 cup walnuts, pecans, almonds, hazelnuts, pistachios, pine nuts, Brazil nuts, macadamia nuts, cashews, or peanuts (changes taste)
1 cup dried fruit (folded into the batter)	1 cup of any of the following: • Dried cherries • Dried cranberries • Dried blueberries • Raisins • Dried currants (smaller and a bit drier)
1 cup dried pumpkin seeds (pepitas)	• 1 cup sunflower seeds
1 tablespoon sesame seeds	• 1 tablespoon finely chopped almonds • 1 tablespoon finely chopped peanuts • 1 tablespoon poppy seeds (white or black)

INDEX

Underscored page references indicate sidebars, tables, and recipe tips. **Boldface** references indicate photographs.